Michaela Thaler

Photocopiable activities for young learners of English

By Jon Marks

Contents

	Page
Introduction	4
General activities	6
Puzzle activities	10

Title	Language	
1 The alphabet	the English alphabet letter formation skills	10
2 English words	some basic vocabulary getting used to writing in English	12
3 Names	the verb *to be*	14
4 Colours	colours	16
5 Who is it?	simple present sentences with adjectives	18
6 Numbers	*there is/there are* numbers 1 - 10 animal vocabulary plural *s*	20
7 Kites	*have got* position of adjectives	22
8 A family	family vocabulary possessive *'s*	24
9 Can the monkey have the banana?	*can/can't* food	26
10 Animal quiz	question forms with *do*, *have got* and *can* animal vocabulary	28
11 Parts of the body	body parts	30
12 Can you see it?	spelling general vocabulary practice for a Starters format	32
13 What are they wearing?	clothes vocabulary present continuous	34
14 What do the teachers want?	imperatives classroom instructions	36
15 Here and now	present continuous *there is/there are* practice for a Starters format	38

16	What's this?	*this* practice for a Starters format	40
17	Mirror writing	phrases and expressions	42
18	Crossword	*and/or, some, there is* articles (*a/an/the*) *do/does, have got*	44
19	Find the word	spelling practice for a Starters format	46
20	What are they doing?	present continuous verbs	48
21	Things in the house	household objects	50
22	Join the dots	food and drink	52
23	What are they saying?	grammar revision	54
24	Listen to the word	pronunciation practice	56
25	What's the word?	vocabulary revision	58
26	Monkey classroom	vocabulary practice	60
27	On the phone	revision of questions and expressions	62
28	What am I?	practice for a Starters format	64
29	Listening puzzle	prepositions of place practice for a Starters format colours, animals	66
30	Stairs	vocabulary practice	68

Mini-puzzles 70

Teacher's notes 70

Title		Language	
31	a or an	*a/an*	72
32	Whose is it?	possessive *'s*	73
33	this, that, these, those	*this/that/these/those*	74
34	Zig	interrogatives: *where/which/what/who/whose*	75
35	Thanks, Mother!	pronunciation of *th*	76
36	Where's the bird?	prepositions of place	77
37	The word is ...	adverbs	78

Grammar and vocabulary index 79

Introduction

Aims

The puzzles in this book are for young learners between 7 to 10 years. They are easy to use, and have a number of aims:

Motivation

Puzzles are fun. They are graphic, attractive and an enjoyable challenge to complete. Pupils enjoy being able to complete a puzzle in another language.

Learner autonomy

Pupils benefit from developing their own skills and strategies for learning. When young learners are completing one of these puzzles, they are discovering their strengths and weaknesses in English. They are finding gaps in their knowledge, and developing and using skills to fill those gaps.

Classroom management

A whole lesson can be a very long time to expect young learners to focus their attention on the teacher - often their attention wanders and they start chatting in their mother tongue. The puzzles in this book allow pupils to work on their own, and aim to be absorbing and fun. As such, they help to keep the classroom atmosphere constructive, focused and conducive to learning.

Using the puzzles

The puzzles can be incorporated into a classroom lesson in a variety of ways:

As a basis for a whole lesson

1. Choose a puzzle which is the right level for your class and which contains at least some language which will be new to them.

2. The Teacher's Notes facing each puzzle contain additional activities for both introducing and following up the puzzle. As a rough guide, using the puzzle plus all the activities in the accompanying Teacher's Notes will take 25 - 40 minutes.

3. If you wish to expand the lesson further, select one or more activities from the General Activities section following this Introduction. These games and activities can be used to practise a wide range of language, and so can be used for further practice of the language of the puzzle. They can also be used to *extend* the language of the puzzle. For example, if a puzzle contained twelve items of food vocabulary, you could use a general activity to revise those twelve items, and to introduce and practise a further six.

As part of a lesson

The puzzles mostly cover themes which are very common in coursebooks. Some have vocabulary aims (e.g. parts of the body) while others focus on grammar (e.g. the simple past). The puzzles and follow-up activities can be slotted into lessons with the same theme, preferably at the end, when learners are familiar with most, or all, of the language they will need for the puzzle.

The syllabus on which these puzzles are based (see page 5) may not match perfectly the syllabus of your course material: the Teacher's Notes to each puzzle contain suggestions for introducing/checking the necessary language before commencing the puzzle.

End-of-lesson 'reward'

A popular way of organising young learners' lessons is to divide them into two parts. The first, which constitutes the bulk of the lesson, is specific in its language aim - perhaps a coursebook unit taught more or less as directed in the teacher's notes. This is followed with a more general, revision-based game or activity which students often interpret as being a 'reward' for having worked well in the first part of the lesson. These activities typically include quizzes, hangman, and other favourite games. Some of the puzzles in this book have general revision aims (and, of course, the required element of fun) and can be used in such an end-of-lesson slot. The Teacher's Notes for some of the puzzles contain ideas for using them as team games.

Homework

Teachers have differing opinions on whether or not it is a good idea to give young learners homework. For those in favour, many of these puzzles are suitable as homework assignments, especially if the introductory activities are used to set them up in class beforehand.

Preparation for the Cambridge Young Learners English Tests

The puzzles in this book are based word-for-word on the syllabus of the Cambridge Young Learners English Tests i.e. the vocabulary listed in the teacher's notes is the same as you would find in the Tests. Some of them use formats similar to those appearing in the Tests. The syllabus was derived from a survey of a wide variety of young learners course material from around the world, and is intended to be compatible with most young learners coursebooks.

The tests are at three levels: Starters (beginner), Movers (elementary) and Flyers (elementary/pre-intermediate), and the three books in this series correspond to those levels. (Information about the tests is available at www.cambridgeesol.org, or by post from Cambridge ESOL, 1 Hills Road, Cambridge, CB1 2EU, United Kingdom.)

However, the material in this book aims to be equally useful to classes which are not preparing for the Tests.

Using the puzzles in class

Preparation

Preparation for all the puzzles is the same: make one photocopy per pupil. For a few of the puzzles, colouring pens or pencils are required.

Procedure

The puzzles can be completed by groups of 2 to 4 working together, or individually with each learner likely to be collaborating on an unstructured basis with his/her neighbours. When the class is working in pairs or groups, give a copy of the puzzle to every pupil, otherwise all the work is likely to be done by the more able ones.

The teaching notes for each puzzle suggest how to introduce it. If further clarification is necessary, give a demonstration: perhaps copy a small part of the puzzle onto the board, and fill in the solution. Making sure everybody understands the format of the puzzle will be vital to its success as an activity. (To check that everybody has understood, perhaps ask a pupil to explain or demonstrate how the puzzle should be completed.)

Get the class to complete the puzzles in pencil so mistakes can be legibly corrected. If pencils are not available to all, you may like to make one or two extra copies in case anybody needs to start again.

Additional games and activities

The teaching notes for each puzzle contain ideas for additional games and activities. These are 'optional extras' to be used if you think the class will benefit from them. They can also be used to expand the puzzles into full-length lessons (see above).

The General Activities following this Introduction can be used for further expansion, and as emergency 'fillers' if the lesson material is completed unexpectedly quickly.

Monitoring and feedback

Make a note of the problems you observe while the puzzle is being completed. Learners are likely to say the answers out loud as they find them. Are there pronunciation problems? Do any of the grammar structures seem to cause difficulty? Was any of the vocabulary confusing?

When the puzzle has been completed go over any problem areas, perhaps using the following techniques:

- Practise pronunciation problems. Create tongue-twister fun by writing on the board a series of words featuring the problem sound (e.g. *this, that, these, those, mother, father, brother*). Get the whole class to shout it out in unison, then ask individual pupils to try.

- Mime problem vocabulary. For example, mime sitting in an armchair (*What am I sitting on?*), or sleeping (*What am I doing?*). The class shouts out the answers.

- With grammar problems, use the information you collect to help plan future lessons.

- If a class has serious difficulty completing the puzzle, give it to them again at a later date. Their initial reaction may be 'We've done this!', but explain that the aim this time is to do it 100% correctly.

Mini-puzzles

The final seven puzzles in this book are quick, self-explanatory puzzles which pupils can do with little preparation and which will take less time to complete. They can be used for quickly practising the target language, as lesson-fillers or as additions to other puzzles. They are reproduced twice on each page in order to reduce photocopying.

General activities

The following games can be used for further practice of the language featured in the puzzles. For suggestions on how to incorporate these activities into lessons, see the Introduction. (These activities can, of course, also be used in other lessons to practise language unrelated to the puzzles.)

1 Chinese whispers race

Preparation

Before the lesson, write down about 15 sentences which include words, phrases or grammar from the puzzle. To practice *apple*, for example, the sentence could be *Do you like apples?* To practice the present continuous, the sentence could be *The monkey is eating a banana*.

Playing the game

1 Organise the class into two teams. Each team stands in a line.

2 Stand at the back of the lines. Ask the pupils at the back of each line to come to you.

3 Whisper a sentence to them. They return to the back of their respective teams and whisper the sentence to the pupil in front of them. This pupil then whispers to the pupil next to them and so on.

4 Meanwhile, the teacher walks to the front of the lines.

5 As soon as the sentence reaches the front of a line, the pupil at the front puts up his/her hand. Wait until both teams have finished. Ask the pupil who put up their hand first to say the sentence: if it is identical to the one the game started with, that team gets a point. If the sentence is not the same, ask the pupil at the front of the other team. If their sentence is correct, award them a point instead.

Tips

- If anybody whispers loudly enough for more than one person to hear, give the other team a point.

- Keep the score on the board, using team names such as Cats and Dogs.

- If there is an odd number of pupils, add another stage: whisper the sentence to pupil A then he/she whispers it to pupils B and C; they run to their respective teams and continue the process.

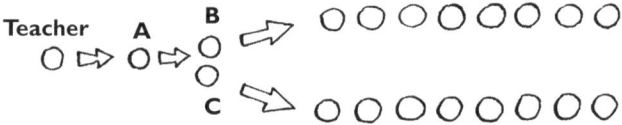

- After a few rounds, get pupils to change their positions in the lines.

2 Back to the board

This version of a favourite ELT game can be used to practice vocabulary with young learners.

Preparation

Make a list of vocabulary. This should include most of the words from the puzzle, plus plenty of other words which the class has learned. Make sure it is possible to mime all the words.

Playing the game

1 Put a chair in front of the board. Organise the class into two or three teams.

2 Get a member of Team A to come and sit on the chair. He/she must not look round at the board. Write three words on the board.

3 The other members of Team A must mime the first word. When the pupil in front of the board guesses it (or gives up), they move on to the next word, and so on. The turn lasts for one minute.

4 Award Team A one point for each word correctly guessed. Then it is Team B's turn, and so on.

Tips

- Keep the score on the board, using team names such as Apples and Bananas.

- Make sure your choice of vocabulary is fair - if one team feels their words are more difficult, they may complain vigorously.

- Continue playing until everybody has had at least one turn at the board.

Variations

- Let everybody mime, instead of just the team mates of the pupil at the board.

- In the adult version of the game, teams define the words on the board, rather than miming them. This may work for older, higher level groups of young learners.

3 Simon says

A popular game which can be used to practise parts of the body and other vocabulary.

Playing the game

1 Get the class to stand up. Introduce the word touch. Practise a few commands such as *Touch your arm, Touch your ear*.

2 Then explain they must do the command only if it is preceded by the words *Simon says*.

3 Give further commands, some with and some without *Simon says*. Anybody who accidentally follows a command not preceded by *Simon says* is out. The last player remaining in the game is the winner.

Variation

With higher level groups, use commands based on miming target vocabulary: *drive a car, eat a pizza, be a monkey, read a book*, etc.

4 Disappearing elephant

This is an adaptation for young learners of the ever-popular game 'Hangman'.

Preparation

Make a list of vocabulary. This should include most of the words from the puzzle, plus plenty of other words which the class has learned.

Playing the game

1 Draw a picture of an elephant on the board like this:

2 Choose a word from your list. Write a line for each letter on the board. Ask pupil A to guess a letter. If the letter is in the word, write it in the appropriate space. If the letter is not in the word, write it elsewhere on the board, and rub out one part of the elephant (begin with the trunk, then the eye, then the mouth, then the ear, then the head, etc.)

3 Next it is pupil B's turn and so on. Anybody can put up their hand at anytime and guess the word (but shouting out is not allowed).

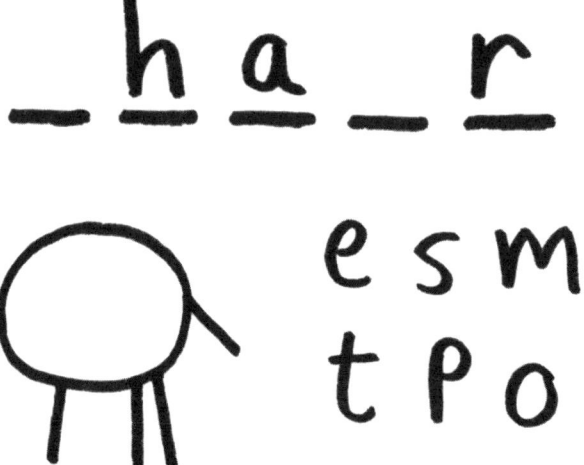

4 If nobody has guessed the word when all the parts of the elephant have disappeared, reveal the word and start again with another word. If a pupil guesses the word correctly, he/she has won that round.

Variation

Instead of a word, the game can be used to practise sentences. These should be fixed phrases such as *What time is it?* On the board, write the first word, and spaces for the remaining words.

The game then proceeds as described above, but with the class suggesting words rather than letters.

5 DIY bingo

A student-centred version of bingo.

Playing the game

1 Get the class to brainstorm vocabulary from the topic featured in the puzzle (e.g. 'Things you can eat'). Write the words on the board.

2 Then draw this grid on the board for pupils to copy.

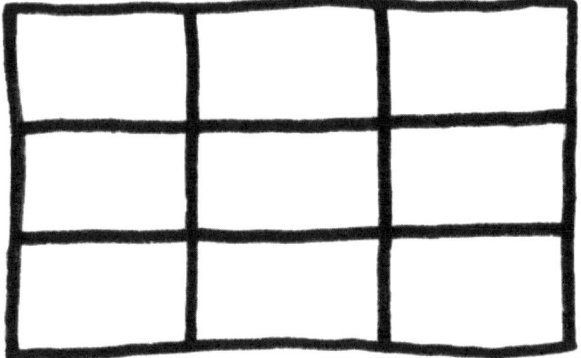

3 Each pupil chooses nine of the words to write into his/her grid.

4 Pupil A chooses a word from her/his grid and calls it out. He/she can cross out the word, as can other pupils who have the word in their grids. Then it is pupil B's turn to call out a word, and so on.

5 The first pupil to cross out all his/her words is the winner.

6 Walking dictation

An activity which can be used to practise any language.

Preparation

On a piece of paper write ten or so sentences featuring the target language (e.g. sentences in the present continuous).

Playing the game

1. Divide the class into two teams. If necessary, move the tables to the walls. The teams stand at one end of the classroom (not too close together). At the other end there is the sheet of paper containing the sentences.

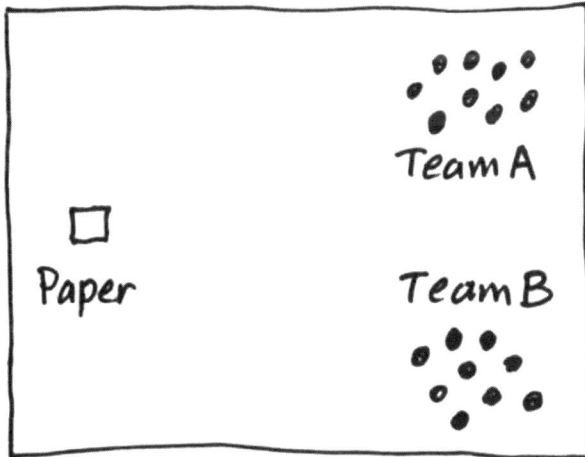

2. A member of each team walks as fast a possible to the paper, memorises a sentence, returns to his/her team, and dictates the sentence. For safety reasons, they are not allowed to run!

3. Then another team member has a turn, and so on. Monitor, and disallow any incorrect sentences (the team member must go back and try again).

4. The first team to collect a full set of sentences wins.

7 Jumbled sentences

This game can be used to practise word order.

Playing the game

1. Divide the class into two or more teams.

2. Select some sentences containing the target language (e.g. questions beginning with *do* and *does*). Concealing what you are doing with a piece of paper, write the first sentence on the board with the words in the wrong order:

you   ice-cream   like   do?

3. Reveal the words. The first team to say the sentence in the correct order wins a point. Continue with further sentences.

8 Anagrams

This is the same as game number 7 above, but instead of guessing jumbled sentences, teams try to solve anagrams of individual words.

9 Memory test

1. Organise the class into groups of three or four.

2. Write examples of the target language on the board. This could be about 15 words from a vocabulary group (e.g. things to eat and drink) or about 8 short sentences (e.g. short questions beginning with *What*).

3. Give the pupils about a minute to memorise the language, then wipe the board clean.

4. Each team must write down as many of the items as they can remember. The team that remembers the most items wins.

10 Spelling competition

1. After a puzzle has been completed, get the class to put their copies of the puzzle away.

2. Dictate about ten words from the puzzle. The pupil who spells the highest number of words correctly is the winner.

1 The alphabet

Language aims

- the alphabet
- letter formation skills

Procedure

1 Write some words or names familiar to the class on the board. Point to a letter, say the letter, then get the class to repeat it. Continue with further letters. (The sounds of the alphabet are a good introduction to the sounds in English words.)

2 Write the whole alphabet on the board. Underline letters *a* to *f*. Say the *a* very quietly, the *b* a little more loudly, and so on, ending with a really loud *f*. Get the class to repeat. Continue with letters *g* to *l*, this time starting loudly and getting quieter. Then go from *m* to *r* starting with a low voice and getting higher. Finally go from *s* to *z* starting slowly and getting quicker.

3 Hand out copies of the puzzle. Pupils work individually to find the shapes of letters and connect up the dots.

Alternative method

Organise the class into pairs, and give each pair a copy of the puzzle. The first pair to find all the letters wins.

Additional activities

1 Making letters from things

Collect together a large quantity of paper clips, counters, jigsaw pieces or any other suitable objects. Set a time limit of 30 seconds. Pupils use the objects to form names or English words which are familiar to them. Whoever makes the most words in the time wins. Repeat as required.

2 Teams form letters

Clear a space in the classroom. Organise the class into two or more teams (there must be at least 10 in each team). Say a letter. The members of each team must organise themselves so that they are standing in the shape of that letter. The first team to do this wins a point.

3 Pupils form letters

Everybody stands up. Say a letter. Everybody must make their body into a shape which looks like that letter.

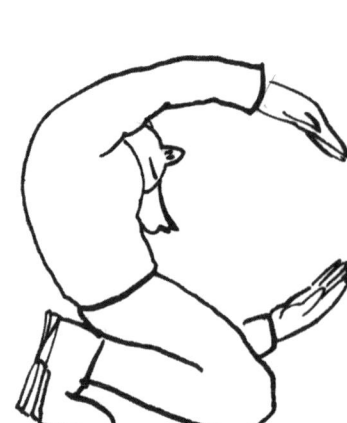

The alphabet

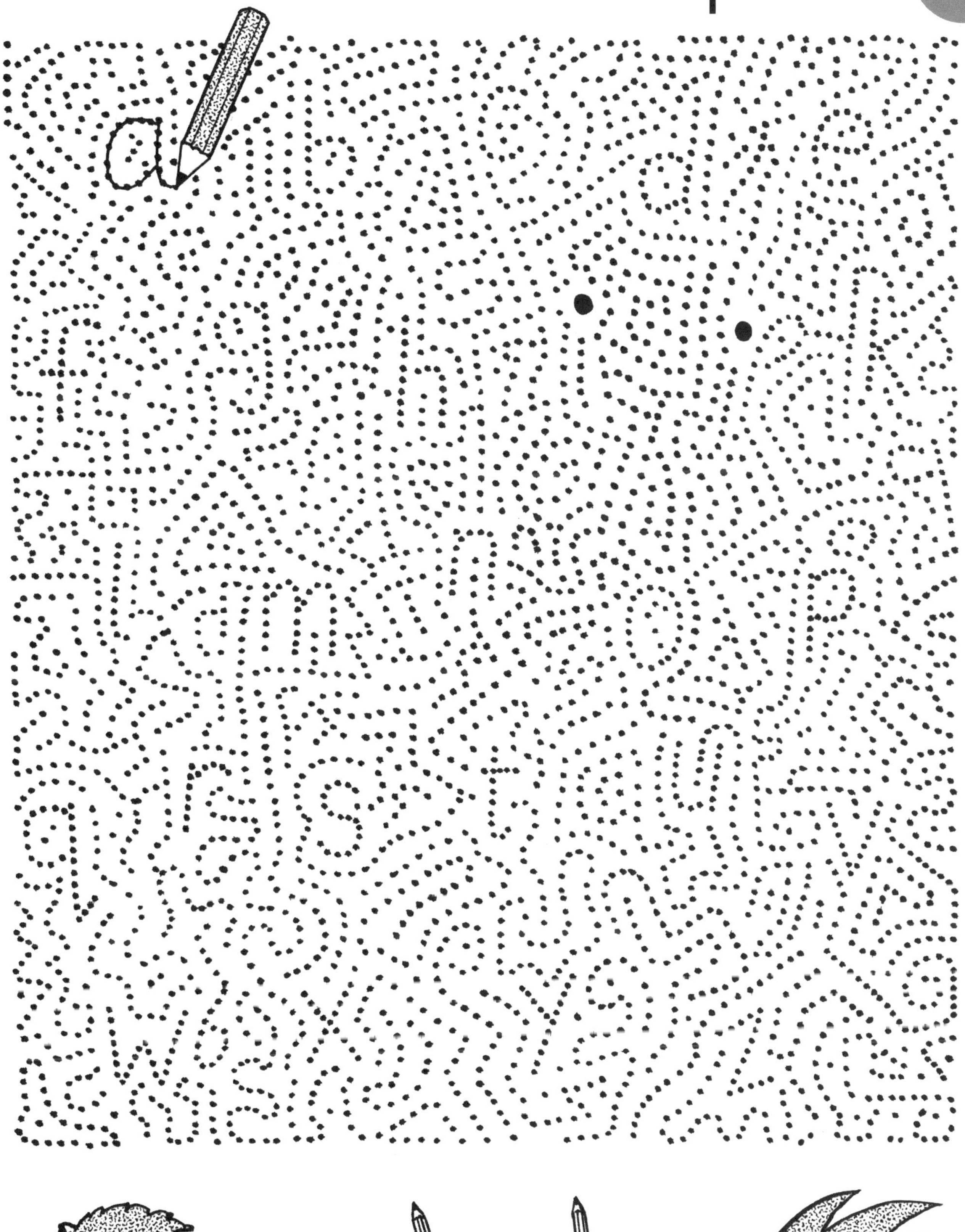

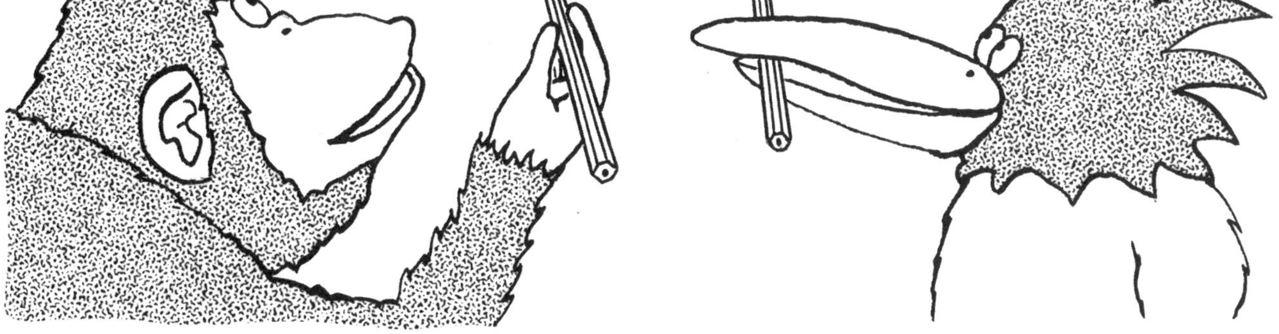

2 English words

Language aims

- basic vocabulary items
- writing in English

Vocabulary

- *cat, banana, dog, computer, apple, pen, robot, house, pencil, jeans, elephant, ball*

Procedure

1 Give out copies of the puzzle.
2 Pre-teach/check the vocabulary in the puzzle: hold up a copy, point to one of the items, and ask, *What's this?* (*It's a dog.*) Do the same with the other items, and repeat until everybody seems confident saying the words.
3 Pupils do the puzzle.
4 Write the answers on the board, or get a succession of pupils to do it. If practical, look at everybody's worksheet to check their answers.

Key

cat

banana

dog

computer

apple

pen

robot

horse

pencil

jeans

elephant

ball

Additional activities

1 More words

Divide the class into two or more teams. Select a word from the coursebook you use. Write it on the board using the same method of jumbling as the puzzle. The first team to guess the word correctly wins a point. Continue with further words.

2 Make your own puzzle

Working in pairs or individually, the class make their own worksheets using the same format as the puzzle. The class could choose words from their coursebooks, or from words you have written on the board. (Perhaps limit the number of words in each puzzle to six or seven.) When they have finished, they exchange with other pupils/pairs and complete each other's puzzles.

3 Bingo

Each pupil chooses six of the items on the puzzle, and puts a circle around each of them. Call out the items at random: if a pupil has circled the object you call, he/she can cross it off. The first pupil to cross off all six chosen items is the winner.

English words 2

cat .... cat

banana ....

dog ....

computer ....

apple ....

pen ....

robot ....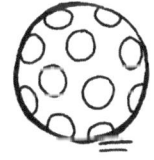

house ....

pencil ....

shoes ....

elephant ....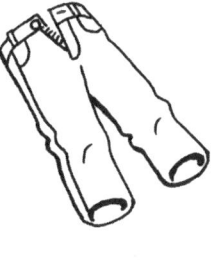

ball ....

3 Names

Language aim

- *to be*

Structures

- *I am, he/she is, they are, we are, Who are you?*

Procedure

1 Draw seven simple faces on the board, and write the following names under them: Tom, Nick, Sam, Sue, Ann, Bill, Ben. Point to the faces and to people in the room, and make statements such as *He is Bill, They are Nick and Ann, I am Ben, We are Ann and Sue*. Some of the statements should be true and some false. After each statement, the class must shout out *yes* or *no* accordingly.

2 Give out copies of the puzzle for pupils to complete. They first draw matching lines between the speech bubbles and the characters they describe (using the t-shirts on the clothes line to help them identify the characters). Then they complete the phrases below.

Key

They are Bill and Ben.

He is Nick.

They are Sam and Sue.

He is Tom.

She is Ann.

Additional activity

For each pupil you will need a piece of paper and a piece of sticky tape. Write the name of one member of class on each piece of paper. Stick one of these name tags on the back of each pupil, making sure that everybody has somebody else's name. Pupils then circulate, asking each other *Am I...?* and getting the answer *yes* or *no*. Once a pupil gets a *yes* answer, he/she sits down. This continues until everybody is seated.

4 Colours

Language aim

- colours

Vocabulary

- *black, blue, brown, green, grey, orange, pink, purple, red, white, yellow*

Starters focus

The puzzle features all the colours from the Starters syllabus.

Procedure

1 Each pupil will need colouring pens/pencils. Introduce/check colours by pointing to things in the room, and asking the class to shout out their colours.

2 Hand out copies of the puzzle. Students colour the picture as directed. When it is coloured it will reveal a bowl of fruit. (You could also use this to practise fruit vocabulary.)

Alternative method

Organise the class into pairs, and hand out copies of the puzzle. The first pair to correctly identify the hidden picture wins.

Additional activities

1 **Clothes bingo**

(This activity is not suitable for classes wearing uniform.) Each pupil chooses five colours, and writes them down. Call out the name of a person in the class, for example, *Maria*. Students can cross off all the colours in their list that Maria is wearing. Then call out the name of another pupil, and so on. The first pupil to cross off all five of their colours is the winner. Repeat as required.

2 **Yes or No?**

Use colours to revise previously-taught vocabulary: call out sentences such as *Bananas are yellow* (the class says *Yes!*), *Elephants are blue.* (*No!*) and *Cars are orange.* (*Yes! - it's possible*).

Colours 4

Colour the picture.

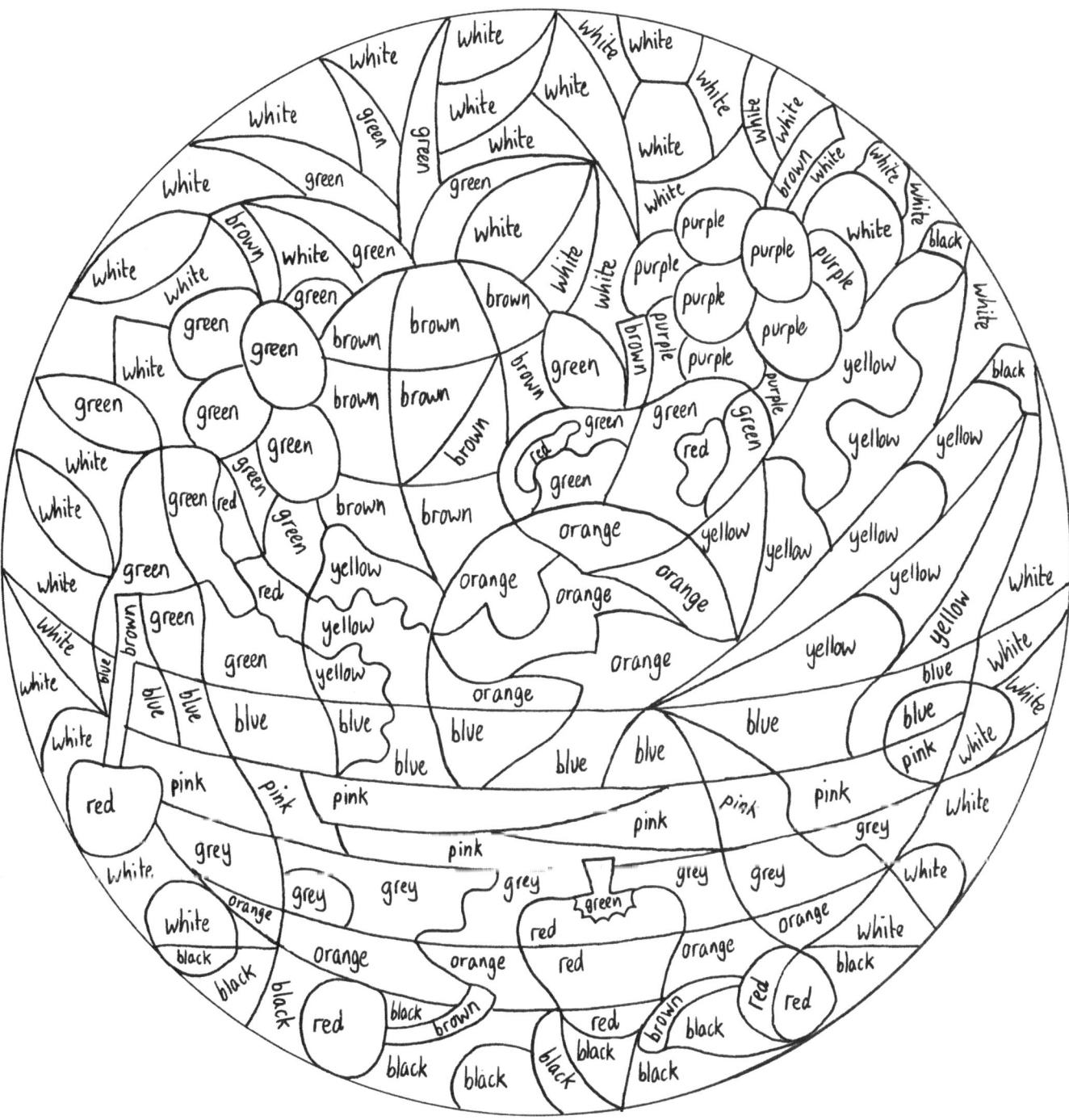

What can you see? ....

5 Who is it?

Language aim

- simple present tense sentences with adjectives

Vocabulary

- adjectives: *small, young, happy, old, big, sad*
- nouns: *boy, girl*
- simple present: *he is/she is, Who...?*

Procedure

1 Introduce/check the vocabulary, e.g. make a sad face, then ask, *Am I happy or sad?* Point to a pupil, *Is she a boy or a girl?*. Repeat with further people/objects to introduce/check *boy/girl, happy/sad, big/small, old/young.*

2 Hand out copies of the puzzle. Read part 1 out loud, and elicit an answer.

3 The class then does the other three parts independently.

Key

1 Ann
2 Tom
3 May
4 Sam

Additional activity

Divide the class into two teams. Ask the following questions about the characters in the worksheet. (the first team to answer each question wins a point).

1 He's big. He's old. Who is it? (ANSWER: *It's Ben.*)
2 He's 10. He's happy. (*Bill*)
3 He's young. He's small. He's sad. (*Nick*)
4 He's big. He's 10. (*Sam*)
5 She's big. (*May*)
6 She's 10. (*Kim*)
7 She's small and happy. (*Ann*)
8 He's small and old. (*Tom*)
9 He's big and happy. (*Ben*)
10 He's young, small and happy. (*Bill*)

Who is it? 5

Ben Sam Ann Tom Bill May Nick Kim

1
She's a girl.
She's small.
She's young.
She's happy.
Who is it?
It's ....

2
He's small.
He's old.
He's happy.
Who is it?
....

3
She's big.
She's old.
She's sad.
Who is it?
....

4
He's a boy.
He's big.
He's 10.
He's sad.
Who is it?
....

6 Numbers

Language aims

- *there is/there are*
- *numbers 1 - 10*
- *animal vocabulary*
- *plural s*

Vocabulary

- *crocodile, cat, spider, elephant, dog, snake, giraffe, monkey, birds, tiger*

Procedure

1. Get the class to count from one to ten. Repeat until everybody seems confident.
2. Write the numbers (in letters) in random order on the board, and get the class to repeat them.
3. Hand out copies of the puzzle for completion. If any of the animal vocabulary is new, answer queries by pointing at the pictures.
4. As pupils get near the end, point out that question 10 is different to the others (*there is* rather than *there are*).

Alternative method

This method also practises colours and pupils will need colouring pens/pencils. Give the following instructions:

Colour the cats orange.

Colour the giraffes yellow.

Colour the dogs brown.

Colour the elephants grey.

Colour the crocodiles green.

Colour the snakes purple.

Colour the monkeys pink.

Colour the birds blue.

Colour the tiger red.

Pupils then complete the puzzle.

Key

2 five
3 seven
4 four
5 six
6 eight
7 two
8 nine
9 ten
10 one

Additional activities

1 One potato, two potato ...

Teach the class the following British schoolchildren's action rhyme:

***One** potato, **two** potato, **three** potato, **four**.*

***Five** potato, **six** potato, **seven** potato, **more**.*

O. U. T. spells 'out', so out you must go.

This is accompanied by an action: groups of up to six put out their right fists, one on top of each other to make a tower. With each word in bold in the rhyme, the person whose fist is at the bottom removes their fist and places it on top of the tower. At the end of the rhyme, the person whose fist is at the top of the pile is out. The remaining players repeat the rhyme until only one person is left - the winner.

2 Animal actions

Pupils take it in turns to mime an animal, while the rest of the class guess and shout out the name (e.g. *It's a monkey.*).

Numbers 6

1. There are ….three…. crocodiles.
2. There are ……………… cats.
3. There ……………… spiders.
4. ……………… elephants.
5. ……………… dogs.
6. ……………… snakes.
7. ……………… giraffes.
8. ……………… monkeys.
9. ……………… birds.
10. ……………… tiger.

7 Kites

Language aims

- *have got*
- position of adjectives

Vocabulary

- adjectives: *big, small, black, white, dirty, clean, old, new*
- nouns: *girl, boy, dog, robot, monkey, bird, snake, cat, monster*
- *have got*

Procedure

1. Introduce/check the adjectives, perhaps by pointing to things in the classroom and asking *Is it big or small?*, *What colour is it?* etc. Elicit answers from the pupils.
2. Hand out the puzzles to the class. Pupils complete by following the jumbled lines and copying the descriptions into the correct sentence.

Alternative method

Divide the class into two teams, and hand out copies of the puzzle. Ask *Who's got the old grey kite?* The first person to put up their hand and give the correct answer wins a point for their team. If members of both teams put up their hands at the same time, give each a point. Keep the score on the board. Continue with the other kites.

Key

2 small black
3 old grey
4 very small
5 dirty white
6 new grey
7 clean white
8 very big
9 big black

Additional activities

1 What is it?

Use the vocabulary from the worksheet to describe an item in the classroom (e.g. for a wastepaper basket: *It's small, green, old and dirty. What is it?*). The class must find and point to the item (it doesn't matter if they don't know the word in English). Repeat as required.

2 Yes or no?

Make statements like the ones below. The class must shout out *Yes* or *No* accordingly.

Elephants are big.

Giraffes are small.

Elephants are grey.

Crocodiles are black and white.

Cats are very big.

Tigers are black and orange.

Giraffes are green and red.

I am old.

Kites 7

a very big kite	a dirty white kite	an old grey kite
a small black kite	a big black kite	a very small kite
a black and white kite	a clean white kite	a new grey kite

1 The girl has got *a black and white kite* ....
2 The boy has got ....
3 The dog has got ....
4 The robot ....
5 The monkey ....
6 The bird ....
7 The snake ....
8 The cat ....
9 The monster ....

8 A family

Language aims

- family vocabulary
- possessive *s*
- *have got*
- position of adjectives.

Vocabulary

- *sister, brother, father, mother, grandmother, grandfather, children, short, long, black, white*

Starters focus

This puzzle contains all the family members vocabulary featured in the Starters syllabus.

Procedure

1. The concept of a family tree may be unfamiliar to the class. Demonstrate by drawing part of your own family tree on the board: *This is me, this is my brother Mario*, etc. Use the family words featured in the puzzle.
2. Hand out copies of the puzzle for the class to complete by writing *yes* or *no*.

Key

1 yes	8 no
2 no	9 no
3 no	10 yes
4 yes	11 no
5 no	12 no
6 yes	13 yes
7 no	14 no
	15 yes

Additional activities

1 Our family trees

Get the class to draw their own simple family trees, using the vocabulary from the puzzle. For each relative, they must write the name, and the relationship to themselves. For example:

Mark

my grandfather

2 Who's in the family?

Introduce the additional vocabulary items *son* and *daughter*. Organise the class into groups of six to eight, preferably with boys and girls mixed more or less evenly. Each group will become a family, and must secretly decide on a family role for each member. For example, a group might decide to become three grandparents, a mother and two children. (If available, dressing up materials could be used.)

Group A goes for a walk round the classroom in the characters of their chosen family members. Everybody else must try to guess which family role each person is *playing* (*Are you a daughter/sister?*) When a pupil's role has been correctly guessed, they sit down. When all the roles have been guessed, it is group B's turn, and so on.

A family 8

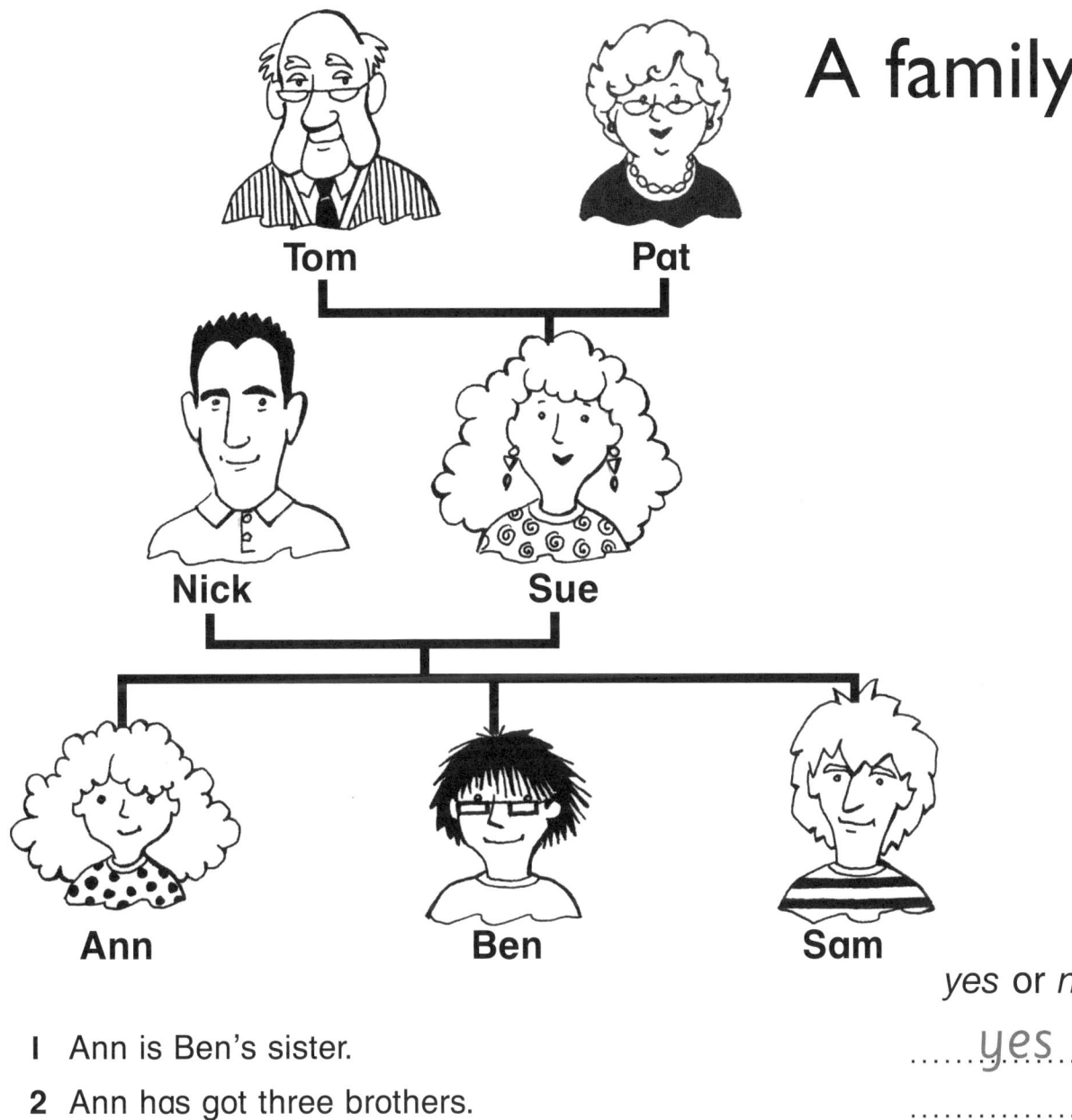

yes or *no*?

1 Ann is Ben's sister. ......yes......
2 Ann has got three brothers. ....
3 Ben's father has got long hair. ....
4 Nick and Sue have got three children. ....
5 Sam's grandmother has got black hair. ....
6 Sue's mother is Ben's grandmother. ....
7 Ann's grandfather is Nick's brother. ....
8 Ben's grandfather is young. ....
9 Sam's sister has got short hair. ....
10 Tom and Pat have got one child. ....
11 Sue's father is Ann's grandmother. ....
12 Ann's brothers have got black hair. ....
13 Ann's mother's mother has got white hair. ....
14 Sam's brother's father has got long hair. ....
15 Ann's brother's mother's children are young. ....

9 Can the monkey have the banana?

Language aims

- can/can't
- food and animal vocabulary

Vocabulary

- have, monkey, cat, horse, dog, pizza, fish, orange juice, apple, ice-cream, meat, cake

Procedure

1 Put an unusual object (for example, a red bag) somewhere in the classroom where some pupils can see it and some can't. Ask various members of the class *Can you see the red bag?*

2 If the class is not familiar with the concept of a maze, hold up a copy of the puzzle, and trace the monkey's route towards the banana. Can he have it or not? (*Yes, he can*). Write *can* in the space in sentence 1 at the bottom of the puzzle. (If you have access to an OHP, this could be done on the screen.)

3 Give out copies of the puzzle for pupils to complete.

Key

1 can
2 can't
3 can
4 can
5 can't
6 can't
7 can't
8 can

Additional activity

What can you feel?

You will need a selection of objects concealed in a bag. Pre-teach (by miming) the word *feel*. Nominate a pupil to close his or her eyes. Give him/her an object. The pupil must guess what it is, and say *I can feel a ....* (They can use mother tongue for the object if necessary.)

Can the monkey have the banana?

Write **can** or **can't**.

1. The monkey ......can...... have the banana.
2. Ann .... have the pizza.
3. The cat .... have the fish.
4. Sam .... have the orange juice.
5. The horse .... have the apple.
6. Tom .... have the ice-cream.
7. The dog .... have the meat.
8. Kim .... have the cake.

10 Animal quiz

Language aims

- animal vocabulary
- simple present tense
- *can*
- *have got*

Vocabulary

- *giraffe, tiger, frog, dog, bird, crocodile, monkey, duck, cow, horse, snake, lizard, goat, spider, mouse/mice, hippo, sheep, elephant, chicken, cat*

Starters focus

The puzzle contains all the animals featured in the Starters syllabus.

Procedure

1 Organise the class into two or more teams. Reading from the puzzle, ask team A a question. If they are correct, they win a point. Then ask team B a question, and so on. Translate any words the class don't know, or draw sketches on the board.

2 Hand out copies of the puzzle for the class to complete. They can do this in their groups.

3 All the animals are illustrated on the puzzle. If any animal vocabulary is unfamiliar to the class, hold up a copy and point to the relevant illustration.

Key

1	Yes	11	No
2	No	12	No
3	Yes	13	No
4	Yes	14	No
5	No	15	No (they've got eight)
6	No	16	No
7	No	17	Yes
8	Yes	18	No
9	Yes	19	No
10	Yes	20	No (not properly)

Additional activities

1 Animal charades

Get a pupil to come to the front of the class. Secretly point to one of the animal illustrations on the puzzle. The pupil must then silently mime that animal, while the rest of the class try to guess which one it is. Continue until everybody has had at least one turn at miming.

2 Animal circular bingo

Each pupil draws six different animals. Pupil A calls out one of his/her animals, and he/she and anybody else who has that animal crosses it off. Then student B calls out one of his/her animals and so on. The first person to cross out all their animals is the winner. Repeat as required.

Animal quiz 10

yes or *no*?

1. Are giraffes brown? ....
2. Do tigers eat bananas? ....
3. Can frogs swim? ....
4. Can dogs swim? ....
5. Have birds got hands? ....
6. Do crocodiles eat fruit? ....
7. Can monkeys talk? ....
8. Do ducks like bread? ....
9. Have cows got brown eyes? ....
10. Have horses got long legs? ....
11. Do cats like dogs? ....
12. Can snakes run? ....
13. Do lizards eat carrots? ....
14. Have goats got blue noses? ....
15. Have spiders got six legs? ....
16. Do mice eat lemons? ....
17. Have hippos got short legs? ....
18. Do sheep eat burgers? ....
19. Can elephants jump? ....
20. Can chickens fly? ....

11 Parts of the body

Language aim

- parts of the body

Vocabulary

- *head, hair, face, nose, eye, ear, arm, hand, foot, feet, leg, body*

Starters focus

This puzzle contains all the body parts featured in the Starters syllabus.

Procedure

1 Practise the vocabulary by pointing to your own head, nose, foot, etc, and getting the class to call out the words. Repeat until everybody seems confident. Write any unfamiliar words on the board, and leave them there.

2 If the class are not used to anagrams, write one or two from the puzzle on the board, and elicit answers.

3 Give out copies of the puzzle. Pupils unscramble the body anagrams next to the monster, and then use these words to label parts of the robot.

Key

eye	hair
face	head
nose	ear
body	arm
leg	hand
feet	foot

1 face	9 nose
2 leg	10 foot
3 hand	11 eye
4 body	12 ear
5 head	13 arm
6 leg	14 ear
7 arm	15 eye
8 mouth	16 hand

Additional activities

1 Simon says

Ask the class to stand up. They must follow your instructions, but only when preceded by the phrase *Simon says...*. Anybody who accidentally starts to follow an instruction not preceded by *Simon says...* is out, and must sit down. Give instructions such as *(Simon says) move your leg* and *(Simon says) put your hand on your ear*. To begin with, demonstrate the instruction as you give it. Later on, just give verbal instructions. The last person still standing is the winner.

2 Picture dictation

Describe a monster for the class to draw. For example, *The monster has got very big ears. He's got three short legs and big feet.* Repeat the activity with pupils taking it in turns to give the instructions.

Parts of the body 11

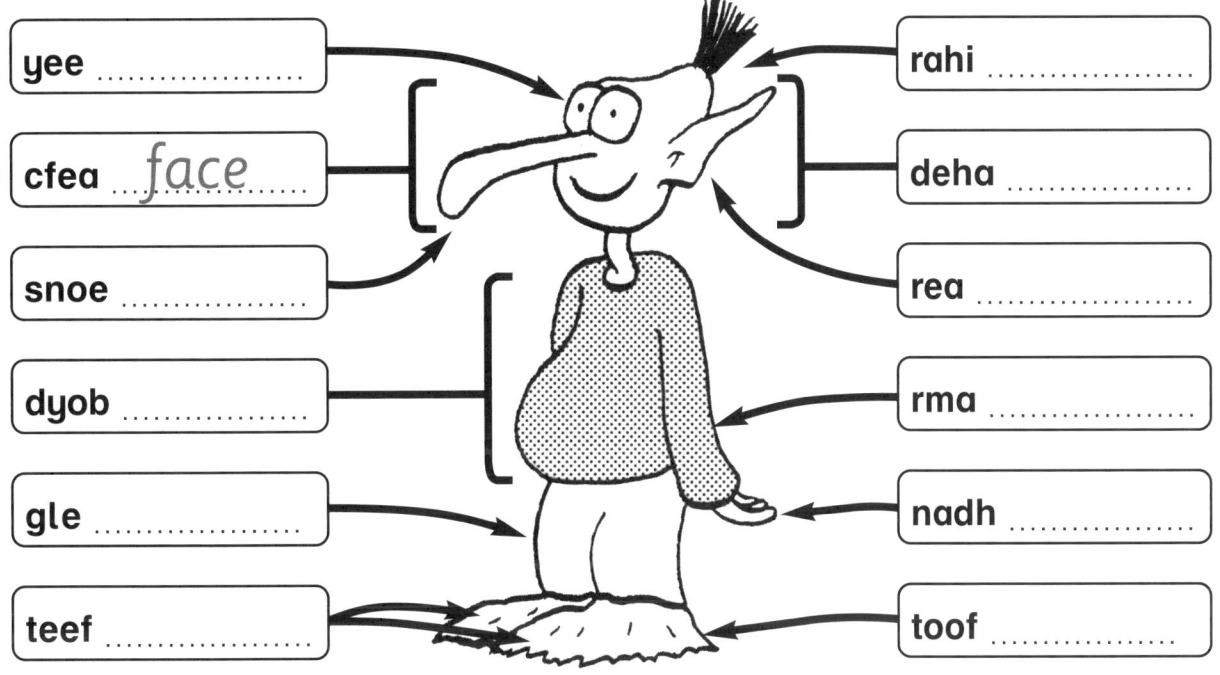

yee ....
cfea face
snoe ....
dyob ....
gle ....
teef ....
rahi ....
deha ....
rea ....
rma ....
nadh ....
toof ....

Help the professor make his robot.

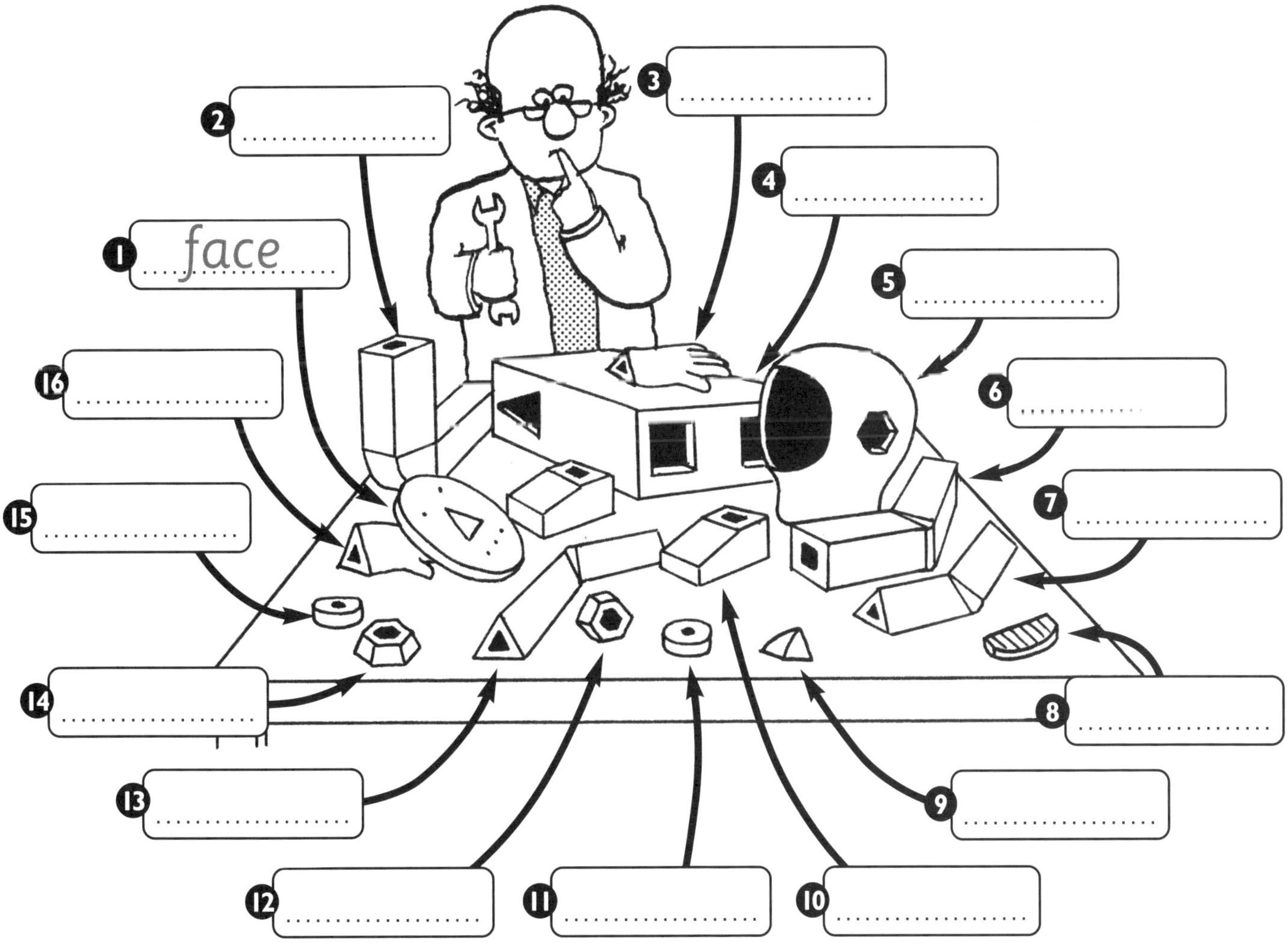

1 face
2
3
4
5
6
7
8
9
10
11
12
13
14
15
16

12 Can you see it?

Language aims

- practice for a Starters format
- spelling
- vocabulary

Vocabulary

- *television, pencil, armchair, bed, helicopter, boat, lamp, guitar, watch, book, ruler, computer, ice-cream, sofa*

Starters focus

This is similar to the format of part 3 of the reading and writing paper.

Procedure

1 Hand out copies of the puzzle. Check that everybody understands what they should be doing: they identify the objects and unscramble the words to write the names. Tell the class to do the ones they can, and to leave the others.

2 Go through the answers with the class together, and write the answers on the board.

Key

1	table	9	ruler
2	pencil	10	guitar
3	television	11	computer
4	armchair	12	watch
5	bed	13	book
6	boat	14	ice-cream
7	helicopter	15	sofa
8	lamp		

Alternative method

Organise the class into teams of up to 4, and hand out copies of the puzzle. The team that gets the most answers within a given time (e.g. 10 minutes) wins.

Additional activities

1 More objects

Divide the class into two or more teams. Draw the first of the objects below on the board. What is it? Team A can have one guess. If they are wrong, Team B can have a guess, and so on. The team which guesses correctly wins a point. Continue with the remaining objects, and add more of your own if you wish.

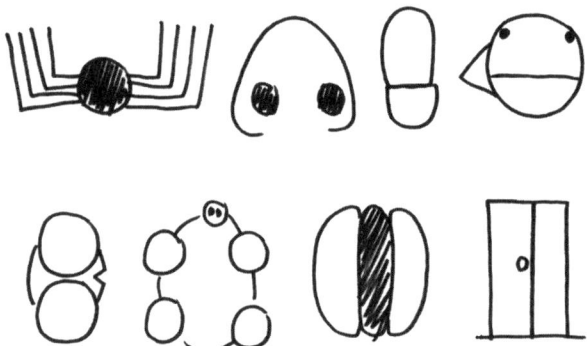

Key

spider, nose, shoe, snake, trousers, elephant, burger, door

Alternative method

Organise the class into pairs/small groups. Give each a photocopy of the pictures above, or project it using an OHP. The pairs/groups must try to identify the objects, and write down the words. The pair/group with the most correct (or plausible alternative) answers wins.

Can you see it? 12

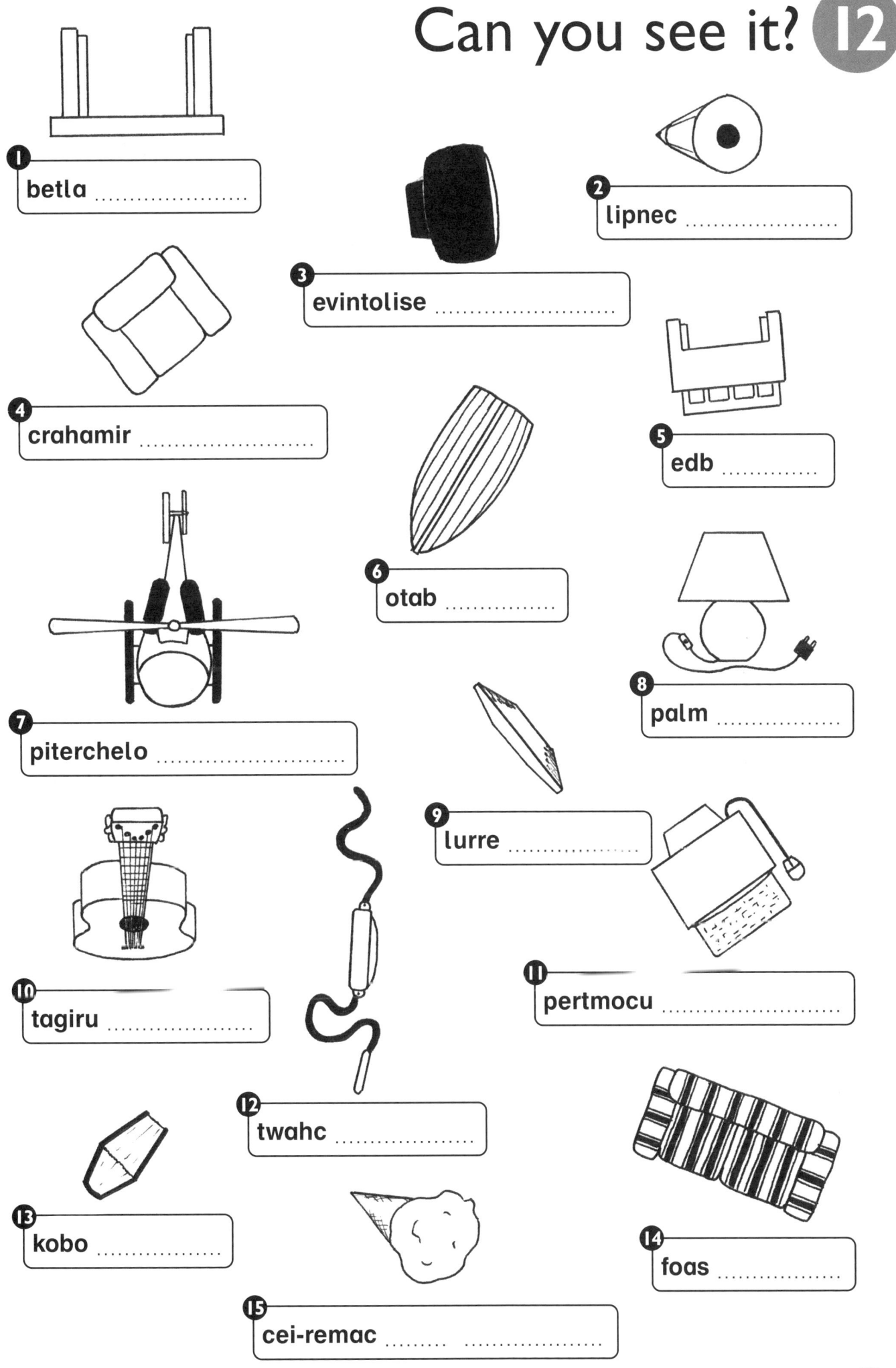

1. betla ....
2. lipnec ....
3. evintolise ....
4. crahamir ....
5. edb ....
6. otab ....
7. piterchelo ....
8. palm ....
9. lurre ....
10. tagiru ....
11. pertmocu ....
12. twahc ....
13. kobo ....
14. foas ....
15. cei-remac ....

13 What are they wearing?

Language aim

- clothes vocabulary

Vocabulary

- hat, jacket, jeans, handbag, dress, glasses, trousers, T-shirt, shirt, shoes, socks, skirt

Starters focus

This puzzle contains all the clothes vocabulary in the Starters syllabus.

Procedure

1. Hand out copies of the puzzle.
2. Hold up a copy, and point to each of the aliens in turn. *What is she (or he) wearing?* Repeat until everybody seems confident with the vocabulary and the pronunciation.
3. Write on the board the words with the more difficult spellings, plus any words which the class didn't know, and leave them there.
4. Pupils complete the puzzle.

Key

Across:

2 jacket
3 handbag
5 glasses
6 trousers
8 shoes
10 skirt

Down:

1 hat
2 jeans
4 dress
6 T-shirt
7 shirt
9 socks

Additional activities

1 Describe a person

Describe a pupil's clothes without mentioning colours, e.g. *She's wearing jeans, a big pullover and an old jacket.* The class must guess who you are describing. Repeat as required. (This activity will not work if the class is in uniform.)

2 Dressing up

If a dressing-up box is available, bring it to the lesson. Arrange the clothes so that they are visible. The students take it in turn to ask for a garment by describing it, e.g. *The green hat.* The class can then wear their chosen garments for the rest of the lesson.

What are they wearing?

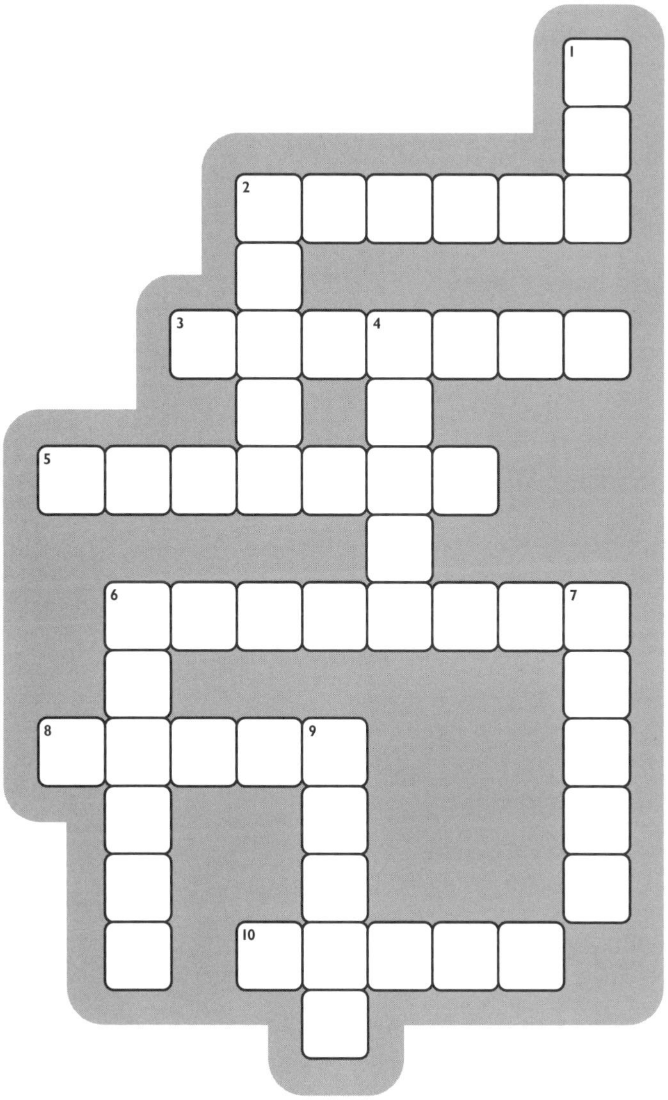

14 What do the teachers want?

Language aim

- classroom instructions

Procedure

1. Give out copies of the puzzle, but tell the class not to write anything yet.
2. Mime one of the instructions from the puzzle. The class has to find the instruction in the list, and call it out. Repeat with the rest of the instructions.
3. Pupils now complete the puzzle by writing the sentences in the appropriate speech bubbles.

Key

2. Open the window.
3. Clean the board.
4. Sit down, please.
5. Be quiet, please.
6. Close your books.
7. Listen to this.
8. Colour this.
9. Draw this.
10. Say that again.

Additional activity

Taking it in turns, pupils mime an instruction from the puzzle, and the rest of the class calls it out.

What do the teachers want? 14

Sit down, please.
Listen to this.
Say that again.
Colour this.
Clean the board.
~~Stand up, please.~~
Be quiet, please.
Open the window.
Draw this.
Close your books.

1. Stand up, please.

15 Here and now

Language aim

- colours
- classroom vocabulary
- *there is/there are*
- present continuous

Vocabulary

black, blue, brown, white, shoes, glasses, T-shirt, socks, girl, boy, board, classroom, desk, picture, wall, bag, floor, clock, book, pen, chair, window, door

Starters focus

This format is similar to part 2 of the Reading and Writing paper, except that the test refers to a picture (usually of a room) rather than using the surrounding classroom.

Procedure

1. Give out copies of the puzzle. Show how to do it by answering the first three or four questions out loud for yourself, e.g. *I am wearing black shoes. No, my shoes are brown. I write 'No' here.*

2. Each pupil then completes the puzzle, answering for himself/herself.

Additional activities

1 All about a pupil

Pick a pupil who isn't shy. Divide the rest of the class into teams of 2 to 4. In turn, each team makes a statement about the pupil, e.g. *She's got black hair.* They can use the puzzle for inspiration. When a team can't think of a new sentence they are 'out'. The last team left in the game wins.

2 Make your own sentences

Pupils write another five 'Here and now' sentences about themselves. They then read these sentences to a partner who has to answer them with *yes* or *no* for himself/herself.

3 Yes or no

Each pupil must write *yes* and *no* on a page of their notebooks like this:

Everybody shuts their eyes. Make a yes/no a statement about the room, e.g. *the clock is grey, Antonio is wearing a blue T-shirt*). Pupils, keeping their eyes closed, must point to *yes* or *no* on their sheets accordingly. Then they can open their eyes. Everybody who was right can award themselves a point. At the end of the game, the person with the most points is the winner.

Here and now 15

yes or *no*?

1 I am wearing black shoes. ....
2 My teacher is wearing glasses. ....
3 I am sitting next to a girl. ....
4 I am sitting between two boys. ....
5 My teacher is standing in front of the board. ....
6 There are two windows in this room. ....
7 There is one door in this room. ....
8 There are nine desks in this room. ....
9 There are some pictures on the walls. ....
10 There are some bags on the floor. ....
11 There is a clock on the wall. ....
12 There are some books on the desks. ....
13 I am wearing a T-shirt. ....
14 I am writing with a blue pen. ....
15 I am sitting on a brown chair. ....
16 I am wearing white socks. ....

16 What's this?

Language aims

- practice for a Starters format
- vocabulary revision and extension
- *this is ...*

Starters focus

This is the format of part 1 of the Reading and Writing paper (except that the illustrations are clear, rather than silhouettes).

Procedure

1 Hand out copies of the puzzle for the class to complete. Check that everybody knows what they are supposed to be doing, i.e. ticking the correct phrases and putting a cross against the incorrect ones. Tell the class to do the ones they can, and to leave the others.

2 Check the answers.

3 Go through the puzzle, getting the class to practise saying *This is a bird*, etc. For the statements which are false, get the class to say, for example, *This is not a potato. This is/It's a banana.*

Alternative method:

Divide the class into teams of up to 4, and hand out copies of the puzzle. The team which gets the most correct answers wins.

Key

1 ✔	10 ✔
2 ✘ (banana)	11 ✘ (cow)
3 ✘ (cat)	12 ✘ (pencil)
4 ✘ (tree)	13 ✘ (sock)
5 ✔	14 ✔
6 ✔	15 ✔
7 ✘ (hat)	16 ✔
8 ✘ (house)	17 ✘ (guitar)
9 ✔	18 ✘ (pear)

Additional activities

1 Shadows

If an OHP or slide projector is available, bring it to the lesson. Set it up so that the beam of light is pointing at a whiteboard or wall. Tell the class it is important not to look directly into the source of the light.

Before the lesson, copy or photocopy and cut up the following cards. (Alternatively, just point to the required word on this grid.)

bird	house	spider	ball
legs	snake	hat	chair
giraffe	plane	tree	elephant
book	egg	crocodile	car

Divide the class into two or more teams. A member of team A comes to the front of the class. Give him/her a card, and whisper a translation if necessary. The pupil then uses the light projector and his/her hands to make a shadow of the object: the rest of the team tries to guess what the shadow is supposed to represent. If they succeed, they win a point. If, after a reasonable amount of time, they have not guessed, the other team(s) have a chance to guess and win a point. Then it is team B's turn, and so on.

Alternative method:

If feasible, close blinds/curtains, and proceed as described above using a torch pointing at the whiteboard or the wall.

2 Outlines

On the back of the copy of the puzzle, each pupil draws a large outline of an object and writes the word for it in English on the other side of the paper. Pupils then take it in turns to hold up their outline while the rest of the class try to guess what it represents.

What's this? 16

1 This is a bird. ✓

2 This is a potato. ✗

3 This is a mouse. ☐

4 This is a doll. ☐

5 This is a fish. ☐

6 This is a monkey. ☐

7 This is a bag. ☐

8 This is a box. ☐

9 This is a spider. ☐

10 This is an egg. ☐

11 This is a snake. ☐

12 This is a rubber. ☐

13 This is a shoe. ☐

14 This is a frog. ☐

15 This is a kite. ☐

16 This is a bus. ☐

17 This is a piano. ☐

18 This is an apple. ☐

17 Mirror writing

Language aim

- introduction/practice of common expressions

Vocabulary

- *Goodbye! Happy birthday! Hello! Here you are. How do you spell ...? I don't know. I like... Pardon? So do I. Sorry. Thanks. What are you doing?*

Starters focus

Using common expressions such as the ones in the puzzle makes a good impression during the Speaking component of the test.

Procedure

1. Write some words on the board in mirror writing. Here are some examples to copy.

    (mirror writing of: yes hello cat)

    Ask the class to tell you what the words are (*cat, hello, yes*).

2. Give out copies of the puzzle. Pupils should first link the speech bubbles with the speakers, as this will help in understanding the mirror writing. They then re-write the expressions. Nobody is allowed to read the speech bubbles using a mirror until the puzzle has been completed.

Additional activities

1 Mirrors

Bring a mirror (or several mirrors) to the lesson. Write three or four sentences on the board. The class must write them in mirror writing. When they have finished, they can use the mirror to check their results.

2 Read the words

Divide the class into two teams. If you feel able to produce your own mirror writing, use it to write a word or phrase which the class has learnt recently on the board. The first team to read it correctly gets a point. Continue with further words/phrases.

3 Mirror messages

Each pupil writes a message for his/her neighbour in mirror writing. They then decipher the messages that have been written for them.

Mirror writing 17

Happy birthday!
Happy birthday!

Hello!

Sorry.

I don't know.

How do you spell 'bike'?

Pardon?

Here you are.

I like ice-cream.

Goodbye!

Thanks!

So do I.

What are you doing?

18 Crossword

Language aim

- revision activity

Structures

- *and/or, some, there is, a/an/the, do/does, have got*

Procedure

1 Tell the class that they are going to do a revision puzzle, and give out copies.
2 Pupils work individually to complete the sentences and then the crossword puzzle.

Key

Across:	**Down:**
2 an	1 this
3 doesn't	2 and
6 hasn't	4 or
9 very	5 there
10 some	7 the
	8 do

Additional activity

Ask the class to make their own crosswords with clues, using the puzzle as a model. The puzzles should be on separate pieces of paper. Set a minimum of five words per puzzle. When the puzzles are finished, collect them in and redistribute them so that everybody has somebody else's puzzle. Pupils then complete the puzzles they have been given.

Crossword 18

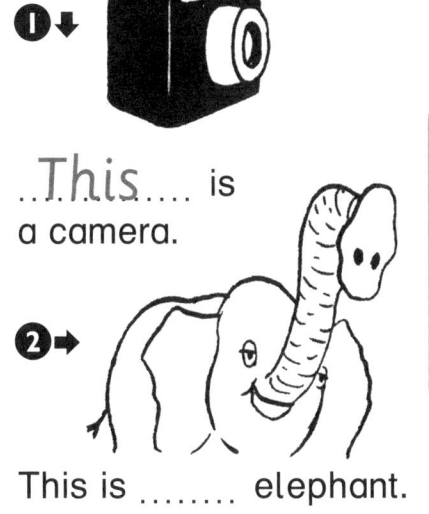

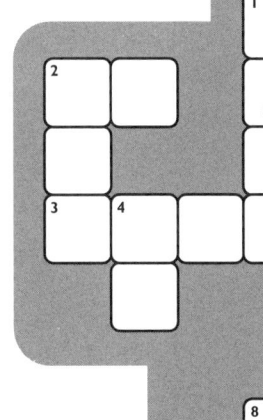

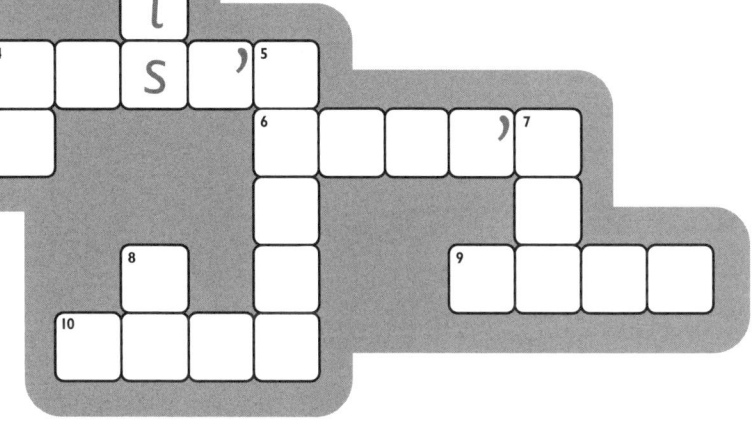

1 ↓ ...This... is a camera.

2 → This is .... elephant.

2 ↓ Tom likes football .... tennis.

3 → Bill .... like coffee.

4 ↓ Is this a cow .... a horse?

5 ↓ .... is a monkey in the car.

6 → Sue .... got a jacket.

7 ↓ The cat is on .... table.

8 ↓ .... you like crosswords?

9 → Ann's face is .... dirty.

10 → Kim has got .... apples.

19 Find the word

Language aims

- vocabulary revision/extension
- practice for a Starters format

Vocabulary

- *chair, clock, car, tree, radio, house, flower, train, camera, behind, under, lorry, cupboard, cross, tick, mirror, motorbike, bookcase, phone, monster*

Starters focus

The format of the puzzle requires similar skills to part 3 of the Reading and Writing paper.

Procedure

1 Hand out copies of the puzzle. Check that everybody understands what they are supposed to be doing: identifying the objects, finding the letters and writing the words. Tell the class to do the ones they can, and to leave any they can't do.

2 Get the class to say the answers out loud and write them on the board.

Alternative method

Divide the class into teams of up to 4, and hand out copies of the puzzle. The team which correctly solves the most clues is the winner (you could give a time limit for this).

Key

1 chair	11 under
2 clock	12 lorry
3 car	13 cupboard
4 tree	14 cross
5 radio	15 tick
6 house	16 mirror
7 flower	17 motorbike
8 train	18 bookcase
9 camera	19 phone
10 behind	20 monster

Additional activities

1 Anagrams

Organise the class into two or more teams. Choose a word from your coursebook, and write an anagram of it on the board. The first team to solve it wins a point. Continue with further anagrams. The team which gets the most points wins.

2 How many words can you make?

Organise the class into pairs/small groups. Write the following letters jumbled-up on the board: **a c d e h l n o p r s t**. The pairs/groups have two minutes to make as many words as they can from these letters (they can use letters more than once if they wish). The pair/team which makes the most words wins.

Find the word 19

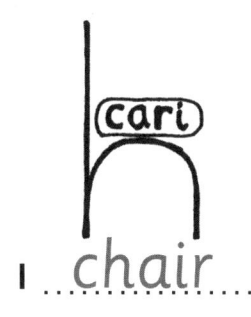

1. chair
2. .... 
3. .... 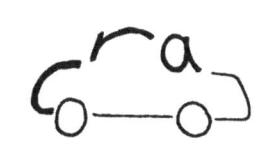
4. .... 
5. .... 
6. .... 
7. .... 
8. .... 
9. .... 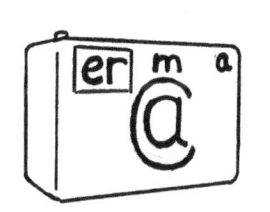
10. .... 
11. .... 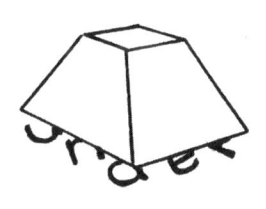
12. .... 
13. .... 
14. .... 
15. .... 
16. .... 
17. .... 
18. .... 
19. .... 
20. ....

20 What are they doing?

Language aim

- present continuous
- verbs

Vocabulary

- *eating, drawing, reading, sleeping, talking, opening, painting, writing, jumping, sitting, pointing, singing, cleaning, phoning, asking, listening, watching, closing, having.*

Starters focus

An important element of the Starters test is connecting sentences in the present continuous with pictures or parts of a picture.

Procedure

1 Hand out copies of the puzzle. Hold up a copy, and point to each monkey in turn. *What is he (or she) doing?* For each picture, elicit the word from the key below. Write in random order on the board any words which seem to be new to some or all of the class, and check pronunciation. Leave them on the board.

2 Pupils then complete the puzzle. Go round helping if necessary, and point out any spelling errors.

3 Finally, students write the mystery sentence in the space provided. (*We are learning English.*)

Key

2 eating	11 sitting
3 drawing	12 pointing
4 reading	13 singing
5 sleeping	14 cleaning
6 talking	15 phoning
7 opening	16 asking
8 painting	17 listening
9 writing	18 watching
10 jumping	19 closing
	20 having

Additional activities

1 Miming game

Organise the class into two or more teams. Mime a verb from your coursebook. Ask, *What am I doing?* The first team to guess what you are doing wins a point. Continue with further verbs. Once the game is established, get pupils to do the miming (whisper or write on a piece of paper the verbs you want them to mime).

2 Silly pictures

Copy or photocopy this grid, and cut up the cards (alternatively, just point to the required sentence). In turns, pupils come to the board, receive a card, and draw a picture to illustrate the sentence. The rest of the class try to guess what the sentence is.

He is eating a book.
She is sitting on a giraffe.
The dog is having a bath.
The elephant is swimming.
She is walking in the sea.
The cat is eating a banana
The bird is watching television.
He is sleeping in a tree.
The crocodiles are playing football.
The fish is flying.
The elephants are jumping.
The teacher is sleeping in the classroom.

What are they doing? 20

What's the sentence?

21 Things in the house

Language aim
- household objects

Vocabulary
- *armchair, bed, bookcase, box, chair, clock, cupboard, door, lamp, mat, mirror, radio, sofa, table, watch*

Starters
Candidates may be required to spell these words 100% correctly in part 3 of the Reading and Writing paper.

Procedure

1 Tell the class you have a list of 15 things you can find in a house. Working in pairs, pupils write down things they think may be on your list. Write your list (the words listed above) on the board, explaining any unfamiliar words and checking pronunciation. Pairs get one point for each item which matches your list and theirs. The pair with the most points wins.

2 Give out copies of the puzzle. Check that everybody understands what they should be doing: they circle or draw a line through the words they find in the wordsearch.

Key

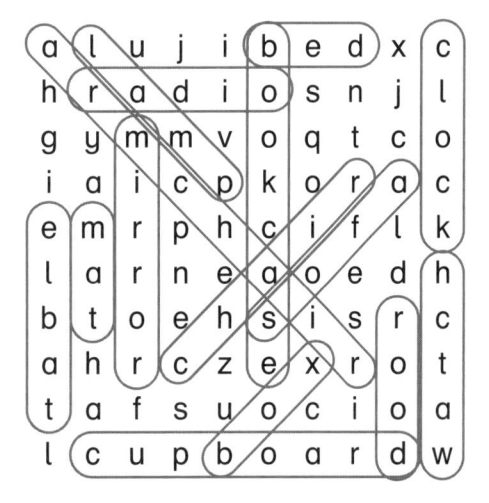

Additional activities

1 Make your own puzzle

Ideally, everybody needs a piece of squared paper. Get pupils to reorganise the vocabulary from the puzzle into a new wordsearch. These new puzzles can then be swapped and solved by another pupil. (Alternatively, tell the class to use a different vocabulary group such as food and drink, or colours.)

2 What is it?

Organise the class into two or more teams. Choose one of the illustrations from the puzzle. Copy one line onto the board, then another, then another, slowly building up the picture. The first team to correctly identify the picture wins a point. Proceed with further pictures. (If you lack artistic skills, it will be an advantage, as it will make the game more challenging!)

Things in the house 21

Find the words.

Look → ↓ ↑ ↘ ↗

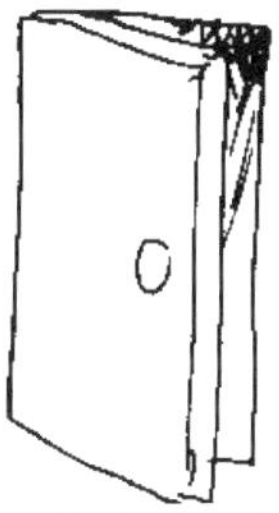

```
a l u j i b e d x c
h r a d i o s n j l
g y m m v o q t c o
i a i c p k o r a c
e m r p h c i f l k
l a r n e a o e d h
b t o e h s i s r c
a h r c z e x r o t
t a f s u o c i o a
l c u p b o a r d w
```

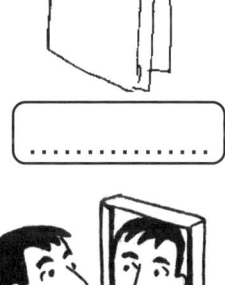

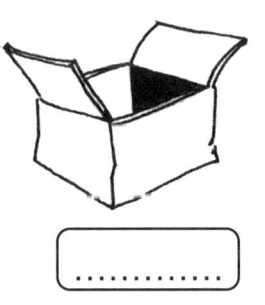

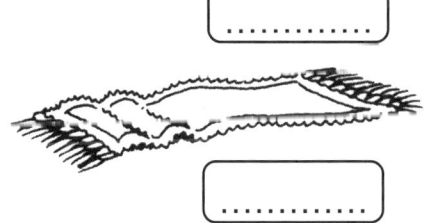

22 Join the dots

Language aim

- food and drink vocabulary

Vocabulary

- *apple, banana, beans, bread, burger, cake, carrot, chicken, coconut, drink, egg, fish, French fries, ice-cream, lemon, mango, milk, onion, orange, pear, pineapple, potato, rice, sausage, tomato, watermelon*

Starters focus

This puzzle contains most of the food/drink vocabulary from the Starters syllabus.

Procedure

1 Choose the words you think will probably be new to the class. Write them on the board in a random order. Next to each, draw a very simple illustration (perhaps copy from the puzzle). Practise the pronunciation of the words.

2 Mime to the class eating/drinking one of the items. The class shouts out the word. Repeat until all the words are being shouted out confidently.

3 Give out the puzzle. Pupils complete it individually, by reading the instructions and joining up the pictures (preferably in pencil). They then complete the sentence at the bottom.

Key

It's a burger and a drink.

Additional activity

Nice or nasty?

Introduce the words *nice* and *nasty*. Give combinations such as: *sausage and bread, carrot and ice-cream, fish and watermelon, coconut and pineapple*. The class has to shout out if they think the combination would be nice or nasty. If there is a disagreement, take a vote. Then get pairs to think up and write down five really nasty combinations.

Join the dots 22

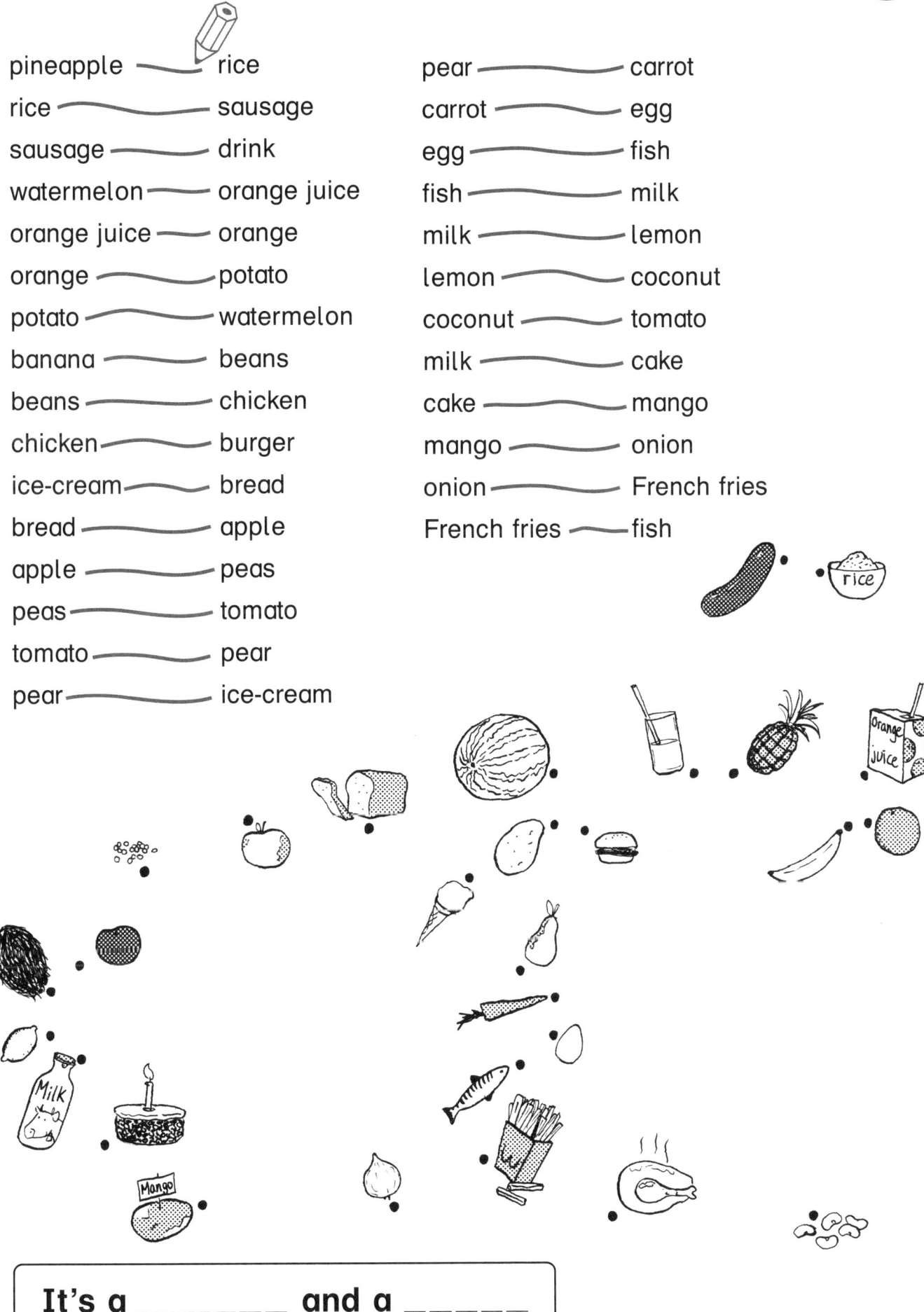

pineapple — rice
rice — sausage
sausage — drink
watermelon — orange juice
orange juice — orange
orange — potato
potato — watermelon
banana — beans
beans — chicken
chicken — burger
ice-cream — bread
bread — apple
apple — peas
peas — tomato
tomato — pear
pear — ice-cream

pear — carrot
carrot — egg
egg — fish
fish — milk
milk — lemon
lemon — coconut
coconut — tomato
milk — cake
cake — mango
mango — onion
onion — French fries
French fries — fish

It's a _____ and a _____

23 What are they saying?

Language aim

- grammar revision

Procedure

1 Give out copies of the puzzle. The task is to find and circle sentences, and then put them into the correct speech bubbles (with spaces between the words). Ask the class to complete the puzzle in pencil, so mistakes can be corrected.

2 Go through the answers with the class.

Key

2 Whose is this?
3 Is it a television?
4 What are these?
5 What are you doing?
6 This is my ice-cream.
7 I don't like milk.
8 I like apples.
9 It's a big plane.
10 I've got a kite.
11 Can I go?

Additional activities

1 Act the sentence

Organise the class into groups of 3 or 4. Each group has to act out all the illustrations in the puzzle. Make it clear that pupils must take it in turns to do the speaking. (Younger classes may lack the cooperation skills required for this activity.)

2 More phrases

On the board, write some more phrases from your coursebook. Pupils must illustrate the phrases with drawings and speech bubbles, as in the puzzle. (Choose sentences which can be illustrated with the most basic of artistic skills.) Display the work on the classroom walls.

What are they saying? 23

Word search grid containing the following phrases:
- Whose is this?
- What are you doing?
- Can I go?
- What's a bike?
- I like apples.
- I don't like milk.
- What are these?
- This is my ice cream.
- I've got a pain.
- It's a television?
- It's Kim.

1. It's Kim.
2. ...
3. ...
4. ...
5. ...
6. ...
7. ...
8. ...
9. ...
10. ...
11. ...

24 Listen to the word

Language aim
- pronunciation practice

Vocabulary
- *wear, no, say, face, two, red, throws, ear, hair, or, they, right, you, me, my, here, clean, door, these, write, nose, know, eye, bookcase, green, head, trees, sea*

Procedure
1. Everybody will need a ruler and a pencil.
2. Check that everybody understands the concept of rhyming words - practise rhyming phrases such as *fat cat, there's a mouse in the house, red bread, sheep go to sleep, look at my book*.
3. Give out copies of the puzzle, but tell the class not to do anything yet.
4. Go round the puzzle getting the class to practise saying the words. Clarify any meanings.
5. Using a ruler, pupils connect the words which rhyme with each other. Doing this will produce a geometric pattern which early finishers may like to colour in.

Additional activity

Rhyming words

Organise the class into teams of 2 to 4. Choose a word from the list below, and say it. Each team then has a minute to think of as many words which rhyme with it as possible. At the end of the minute, the team which has written the most words wins a point. Continue with further words from the list.

bed, tree, radio, chair, those, cat, peas, draw

Key

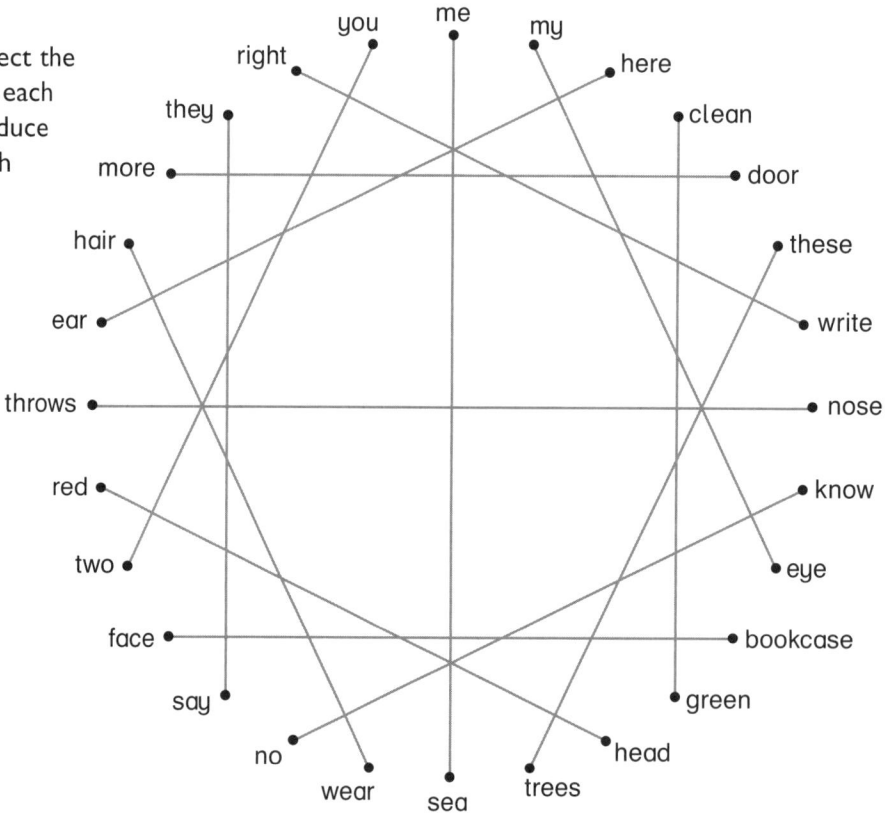

56

Listen to the word 24

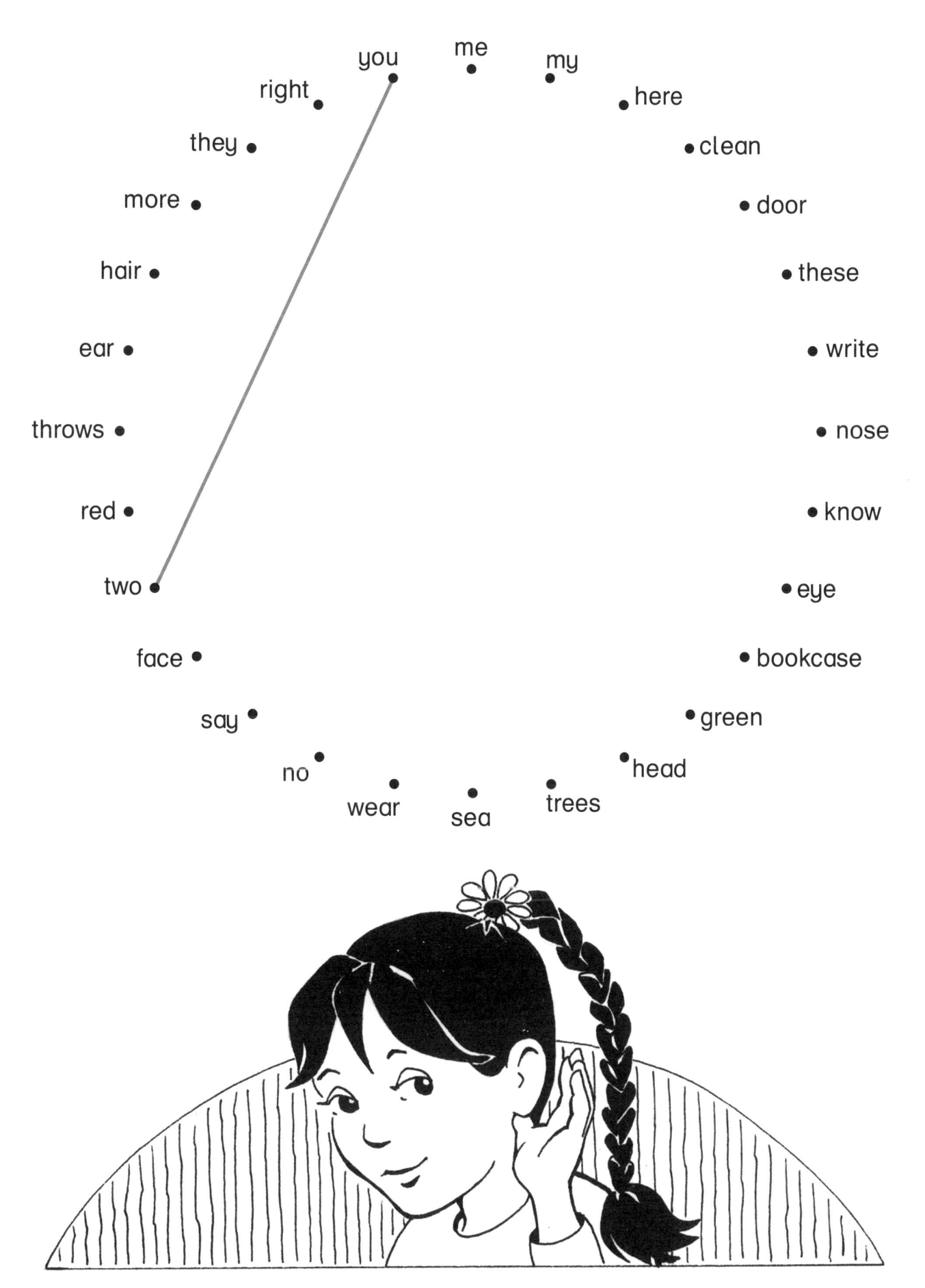

you   me   my
right   here
they   clean
more   door
hair   these
ear   write
throws   nose
red   know
two   eye
face   bookcase
say   green
no   head
wear sea trees

25 What's the word?

Language aim

- vocabulary revision

Vocabulary

- See key below and puzzle

Procedure

1 Write the answers (see key below) jumbled up on the board. (If you want to make it more challenging, add some extra words.)

2 Give out copies for the class to complete. Check that everybody knows what they should be doing: finding words from the written clues.

3 Answer vocabulary queries as they arise.

Alternative method

Organise the class into two or more teams. As an example, read out the clues for number 1, and give the answer. Repeat with 2. Then read out the clues for number 3. The first team to guess the 'mystery' word wins a point. Continue through the rest of the puzzle. Afterwards, hand out copies of the puzzle for completion by the class.

Key

2 football	12 ball
3 book	13 piano
4 television	14 dining room
5 monkey	15 crocodile
6 jeans	16 flower
7 birthday	17 socks
8 watermelon	18 cow
9 bedroom	19 bathroom
10 numbers	20 names
11 snake	21 question

Additional activity

Word clues

Organise the class into two or more teams. Choose a word (e.g. *elephant*) and on the board write a line for each letter (_ _ _ _ _ _ _ _). Then give clues one at a time (*It's an animal, It's very big, It's grey*). The first team to guess correctly wins a point. Repeat as required.

What's the word? 25

1. teacher / lesson / board — s c h o o l
2. sport / play / kick — _____
3. read / bookcase — _____
4. watch / picture — _____
5. banana / ooh ooh ooh! — _____
6. wear / trousers / blue — _____
7. favourite day / How old are you today? — _____
8. fruit / green / very big — _____
9. room / sleep — _____
10. seven / four / nine / one — _____
11. long / no legs / sssssssss! — _____
12. play / game / bounce — ____
13. play / music / hands / black / white — _____
14. room / eat / table — _____ ____
15. animal / green / water / teeth — _____
16. garden / beautiful / colours — _____
17. wear / feet / shoes and ... — _____
18. animal / black or brown / milk — ___
19. room / have a bath — _____
20. Ann / Bill / Kim / Pat / Sue / Sam — _____
21. ask / answer / right — _____

26 Monkey classroom

Language aim

- vocabulary revision/extension

Vocabulary

- *bed, bath, bread, book, ball, bag, bike/bicycle, burger, box, boy, baby, beach, boat, board, bird, bookcase*

Procedure

1 Hand out copies of the puzzle, but tell the class not to do anything yet.

2 Ask the class to put up their hands and point to something in the picture which begins with *b*. Continue until about 8 items have been named.

3 Pupils write these words into the spaces at the bottom of the puzzle, and then look for more words.

Alternative method

Organise the class into groups of 2 to 4. Each group looks for words beginning with *b*, and writes them in the spaces below the picture. The group which finds the most (in a given time) or the first group to find 16 wins.

Key

baby, bag, ball, bath, beach, bed, bike/bicycle, bird, board, boat, book, bookcase, box, boy, bread, burger (total 16)

Additional activity

Vocabulary tennis

Organise the class into two teams. Choose a letter from the list below, and say it. The first member of Team A must think of another word which begins with that letter. Then it is the turn of the first member of Team B, then the second member of team A and so on. When somebody can't think of another word, the opposite team gets a point. Continue the game with further letters.

Suitable letters: *a, c, d, f, g, h, m, p, s, t*

Monkey classroom 26

Find words which begin with **b**

b................	....	....	....
b................	....	....	....
b................	....	....	....
....	....	....	....

27 On the phone

Language aim

- grammar revision
- practice of common questions and expressions

Procedure

1 Hand out copies of the puzzle, but tell the class not to do anything yet.

2 Make the noise of a telephone ringing. Point to a pupil – she or he must pick up an imaginary phone to answer your call.

3 Say the first phrase from the left column (*What's your name?*). The chosen pupil has to answer (*My name's Bill*).

4 Choose another pupil and continue with the next phrase (*Have you got a pen?*). This time the pupil will have to find the answer on the worksheet (*Yes, I have* or *I don't know* are both acceptable).

5 Continue through the phrases with other pupils.

6 The class completes the puzzle in pencil. Although *I don't know* can initially be matched with several of the left-hand phrases, to complete the puzzle correctly, it can only go with *How do you spell computer?*

Key

Have you got a pen? ➡ *Yes I have.*

I like cats. ➡ *So do I.*

Happy birthday! ➡ *It's not my birthday.*

Can you ride a bike? ➡ *No, I can't.*

Are you a boy? ➡ *No, I'm not.*

How do you spell computer? ➡ *I don't know.*

What colour are your socks? ➡ *They're blue*

How many children are there in your class? ➡ *Ten.*

What are you doing? ➡ *I'm talking to you.*

Additional activity

Pick a pupil and say one of the phrases from the left-hand column of the puzzle. The pupil must answer with a different phrase to the one in the puzzle. Continue with other phrases and pupils.

On the phone 27

What's your name?

Have you got a pen?

I like cats.

Happy birthday!

Can you ride a bike?

Are you a boy?

How do you spell computer?

What colour are your socks?

How many children are there in your class?

What are you doing?

So do I.

It's not my birthday.

No, I'm not.

My name's Bill.

They're blue.

Ten.

I'm talking to you.

No, I can't.

Yes, I have.

I don't know.

28 What am I?

Language aim

- vocabulary revision/extension
- practice for a Starters format

Vocabulary

house, sun, bed, milk, bike, bread, picture, chair, hat, hair, book, sea, pea, tennis, water

Starters focus

Part 4 of the Reading and Writing paper is a riddle, in which an inanimate object may ask *What am I?* This puzzle can be used to introduce that concept.

Procedure

1. Give out copies of the puzzle.
2. Read the first two or three questions out loud. Elicit the answers. Point out that all the answers are illustrated at the bottom of the worksheet.
3. Get the class to continue independently. Answer any vocabulary queries as they arise. (To make the puzzle easier, write the answers on the board in a random order.)

Key

2	house	9	chair
3	sun	10	hat
4	bed	11	hair
5	milk	12	sea
6	bike	13	pea
7	bread	14	tennis
8	picture	15	water

Additional activities

1 Challenge the teacher

Working individually or in pairs, the class has five minutes to come up with more 'What am I?' clues. Get the class to challenge you with their riddles (they must also give you the number of letters in the word). For each that you can guess, you gain a point; for each that you can't guess, the class gains a point.

2 Team challenge

Organise the class into teams of three to four. Each team devises at least three more riddles as in the puzzle. Team A then asks team B to solve one of their riddles (they must also give the number of letters in the word). If Team B can't answer, Team C has a chance and so on. The first team to guess the riddle gets a point. If nobody can guess the riddle, it must have been too difficult, and Team A loses one point. Then it is Team B's turn to ask, and so on.

What am I? 28

1 You can read me.   I'm a <u>book</u>.

2 You can live in me. I've got rooms.   I'm a _____.

3 You can't see me at night.   I'm the ____.

4 You can sleep on me.   I'm a ____.

5 You can drink me. I'm white.   I'm _____.

6 You can ride me.   I'm a _____.

7 You can eat me. I'm white or brown.   I'm _____.

8 You can draw or paint me.   I'm a _____.

9 You can sit on me.   I'm a _____.

10 You can wear me on your head.   I'm a ____.

11 You have got me on your head.   I'm _____.

12 Fish live in me.   I'm the ____.

13 You can eat me. I'm green and very small.   I'm a ____.

14 You can play me with a small yellow ball.   I'm _____.

15 You drink me. I haven't got a colour.   I'm _____.

29 Listening puzzle

Language aims

- prepositions of place
- colours
- listening practice
- practice for a Starters format

Vocabulary

- *between, behind, in front of, next to, on, under, lorry, clock, giraffe, cat, robot, jeans, doll, car, monster, snake, bird, spider, apple, red, orange, yellow, brown, pink, red, grey, green, purple, blue*

Starters focus

Colouring instructions are the basis of part 4 of the Listening paper.

Procedure

1 Each pupil needs colouring pens/pencils.

2 Give out copies of the puzzle.

3 Check the vocabulary by holding up a copy (or projecting it using an OHP), pointing to something in the picture and asking, *What is it?* or, *How many snakes are there?* Repeat this until everybody seems confident with the vocabulary.

4 Ask questions using the prepositions of place: *What's on the radio? What's between a pair of jeans and a cat?*

5 Read the following instructions.

*Find a lorry next to a clock.
Colour the lorry blue.*

*Find a giraffe in front of a cat.
Colour the giraffe yellow.*

*Find a pair of jeans between a cat and a robot.
Colour the jeans blue.*

*Find a car under a doll.
Colour the car purple.*

*Find a snake behind a monster.
Colour the snake green.*

*Find a robot in front of a snake.
Colour the robot grey.*

*Find a bird in front of a monster and a snake.
Colour the bird pink.*

*Find a monster under a spider.
Colour the monster red.*

*Find a doll on a car.
Colour the doll pink.*

*Find a cat behind a giraffe.
Colour the cat brown.*

*Find a snake behind a bird.
Colour the snake yellow.*

*Find a snake behind a robot.
Colour the snake orange.*

*Find an apple between a doll and a robot.
Colour the apple red.*

What word can you see?

Key

Hello

Additional activities

1 Simon says

Use the prepositions of place from the puzzle for a round or two of this game. (For the rules, see General Activities section.) Give instructions such as *(Simon says) put your pen under your book* and *(Simon says) stand next to your chair*.

2 Picture dictation

Give the following instructions:

*Draw a small house.
Draw a tree.
Between the house and the tree, draw a man.
Behind the house, draw another tree.
In front of the house, draw a bicycle.
Next to the house, draw a chair.
On the chair, draw a girl.
Under the chair, draw a spider.*

Listening puzzle 29

Listen to your teacher. What word can you see? ....

30 Stairs

Language aim

- vocabulary practice

Procedure

1 Hand out copies of the puzzle.
2 On the board, write one way of completing the puzzle. For example:

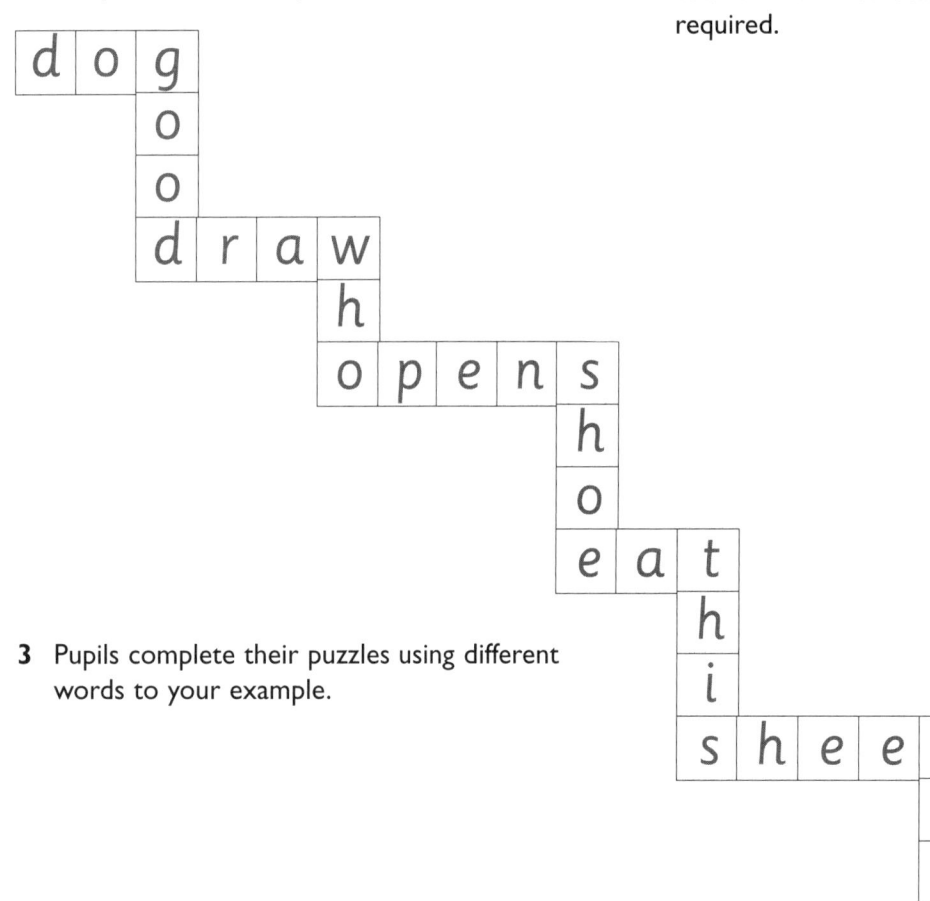

```
d o g
    o
    o
    d r a w
        h
        o p e n s
                h
                o
                e a t
                    h
                    i
                    s h e e p
                            e
                            a
                            r a d i o
                                    l
                                    d
```

3 Pupils complete their puzzles using different words to your example.

Additional activity

Divide the class into two teams. Team A suggests a word which you write horizontally on the board. Then team B says a word which starts vertically down from the last letter of team A's word. The object is to suggest words which are as long as possible. When each team has given five words, count up the letters. The team which has totalled the most letters wins a point. Repeat as required.

Stairs 30

cat two open

apple eat this

red dolls

Mini-puzzles
teacher's notes

31 a or an

Language aim

- articles: *a/an*

Procedure

1 Give out copies of the puzzle, but tell the class not to write anything yet.

2 Go through the puzzle with the class saying each item: *a cat, an apple, an elephant,* etc. Pupils then complete the puzzle.

Key

an elephant, ear, arm, eye, egg

a banana, hand, hat, shoe, leg

32 Whose is it?

Language aim

- possessive *'s*

Procedure

1 Hand out copies of the puzzle, but tell the class not to write anything yet.

2 Check the names of the animals in the illustration at the top of the puzzle. Go through the puzzle eliciting the owner of each tail.

3 The class then completes the puzzle in writing.

4 Go through the answers. Ask the class if anyone has noticed the difference between the pronunciation of *horse's/mouse's* and the other *'s* words in the puzzle.

Key

2 horse's   3 elephant's   4 mouse's
5 crocodile's   6 tiger's   7 cat's   8 bird's

33 this, that, these, those

Language aim

- *this/that/these/those*

Procedure

1 Practise the target vocabulary using classroom examples (*What's this? What are those?*).

2 Hand out copies of the puzzle. Pupils complete it by putting *this*, *that*, *these* or *those* into the gaps in the speech bubbles, and then writing those same words into the relevant boxes in the word puzzle.

3 The vertical shaded column will then read *he_i_o_te_*. Ask the class if anyone can guess the word (*helicopter*). Finally, practise the sentences for pronunciation.

Key

1 that   2 these   3 this
4 those   5 that   6 these

34 Zig

Language aim

- interrogatives: *which, what, who, whose, where*

Procedure

1 Practise the target language using classroom examples (*Where's my book, Which is your pen?*).

2 Hand out copies of the puzzle. Pupils complete it by filling the gaps in the speech bubbles with a *wh* word. They then write these in the crossword grid.

3 Go through the answers, and practise the sentences for pronunciation.

Key

Across: 3 whose   5 which   6 what

Down: 1 who   2 where   3 which   4 what

35 thanks v this

Language aim

- pronunciation of *th*

Procedure

1 Hand out copies of the puzzle, but tell the class not to write anything yet.

2 Practise the words at the bottom of the puzzle (including *thanks* and *this*). Make sure everyone understands that there are two distinct *th* sounds. Continue until everybody is confident with both pronunciations of *th*.

3 Say one of the words again. The class shouts out *thanks* or *this* depending on which column the word should go into. Continue with the other words, then the class completes the puzzle.

4 Go through the answers. Ask the class if anyone can think of any more words with *th*. Which column should these new words go into?

Key

thanks: *mouth, birthday, three, throw, bath*

this: *the, there, they, mother, clothes, with*

36 Where's the bird?

Language aim

- prepositions of place: *in, on, under, next to, between, behind, in front of*

Procedure

1 Practise the prepositions using examples in the classroom.

2 Hand out copies of the puzzle. The object is to solve the anagrams, and then find the words in the wordsearch.

3 Go through the answers. Ask the class to write one sentence about the classroom with each of the prepositions.

Key

```
i n c s y t x i h
u b e t w e e n p
b v r c d w z f a
n e p f m u m r l
e q h d g r e o n
x n h i v d s n k
t w j x n u t t y
t q k u j d v o e
o a f g l h z f j
```

37 The word is ...

Language aim

- adverbs

Procedure

1 This puzzle is intended for classes which are already familiar with most of the vocabulary.

2 Hand out copies of the puzzle. The object is to put the words at the top of the page into the gaps in the speech bubbles, and then write these words in the crossword.

3 Go through the answers, and practice the sentences for pronunciation.

Key

Across: 2 now 4 there 5 again 7 very

Down: 1 today 3 here 6 not

> **Note:** the mini puzzles which follow are reproduced twice on each page to reduce photocopying.

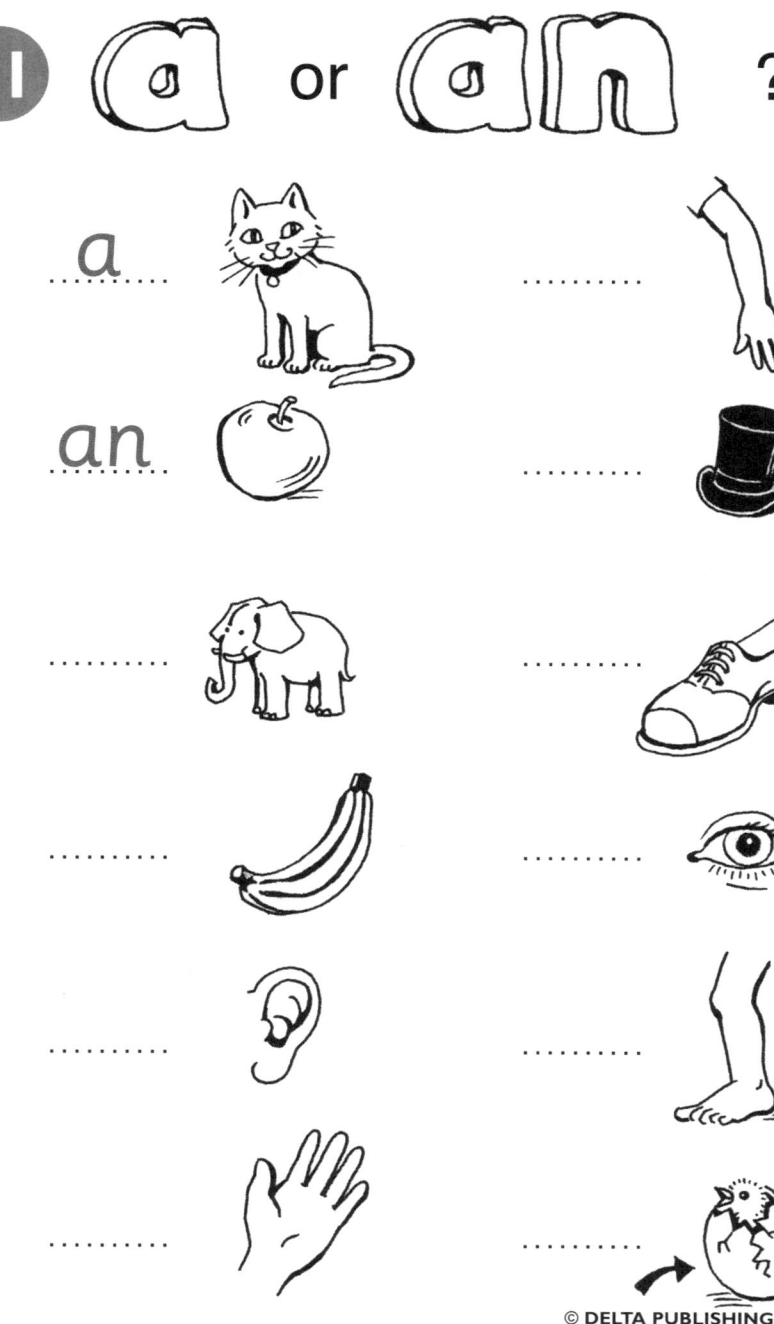

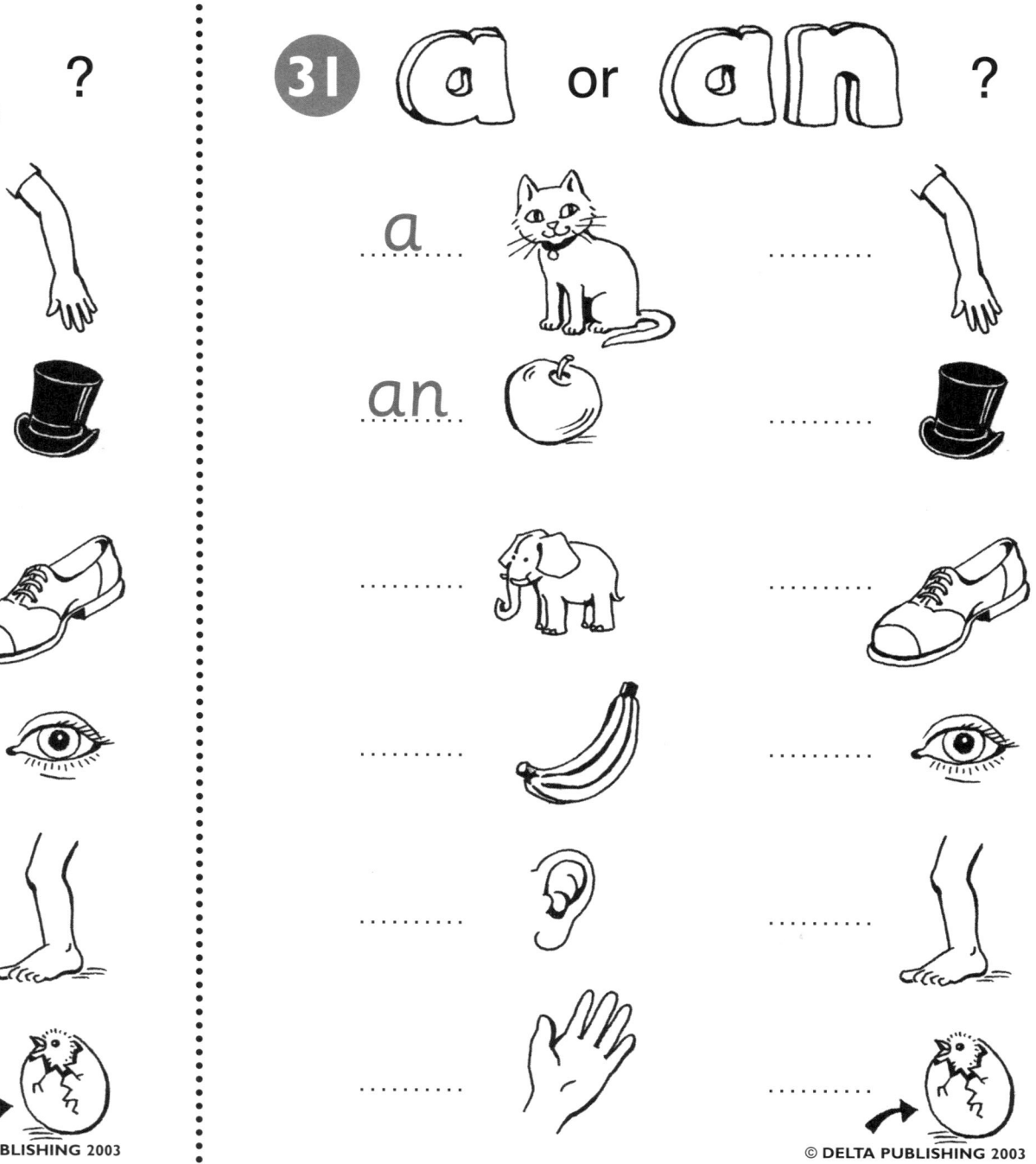

31 a or an ?

a .... (cat)
an .... (apple)
.... (elephant)
.... (banana)
.... (ear)
.... (hand)

.... (arm)
.... (hat)
.... (shoe)
.... (eye)
.... (foot)
.... (egg)

© DELTA PUBLISHING 2003

32 Whose is it?

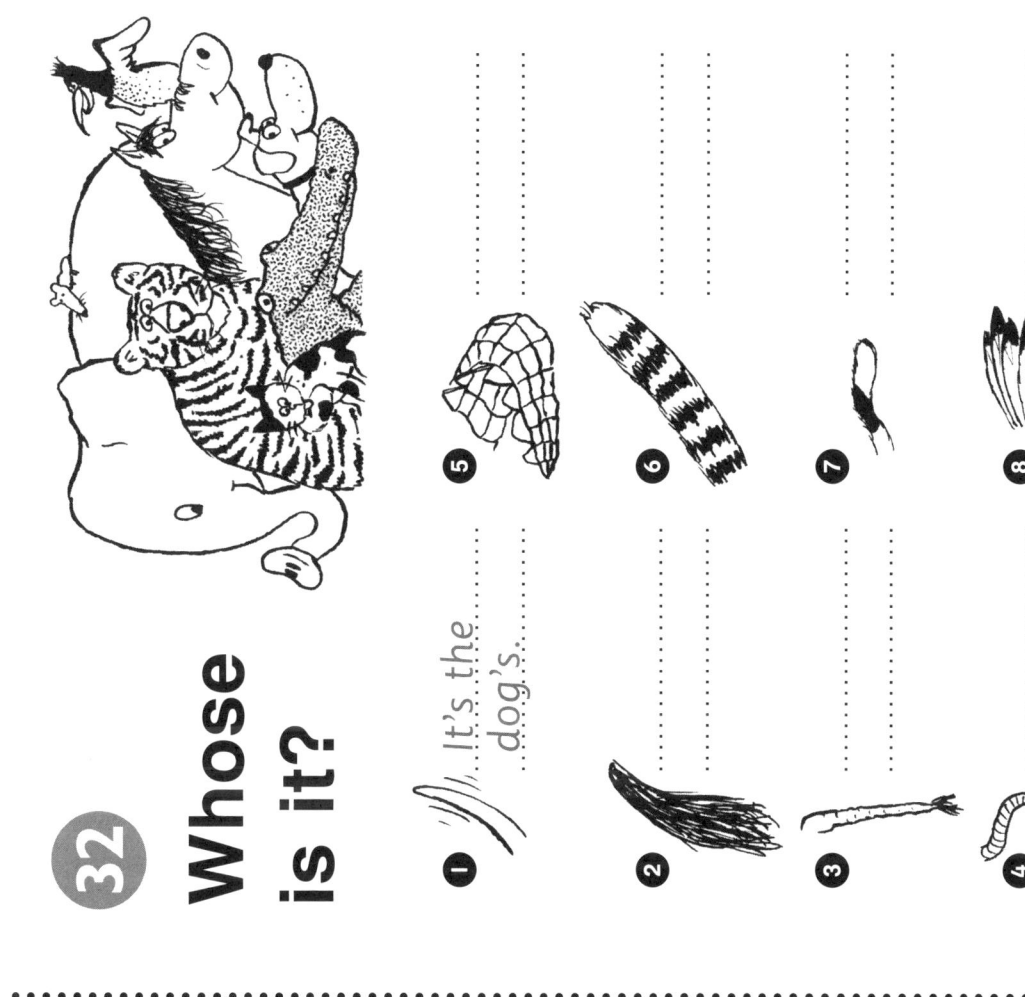

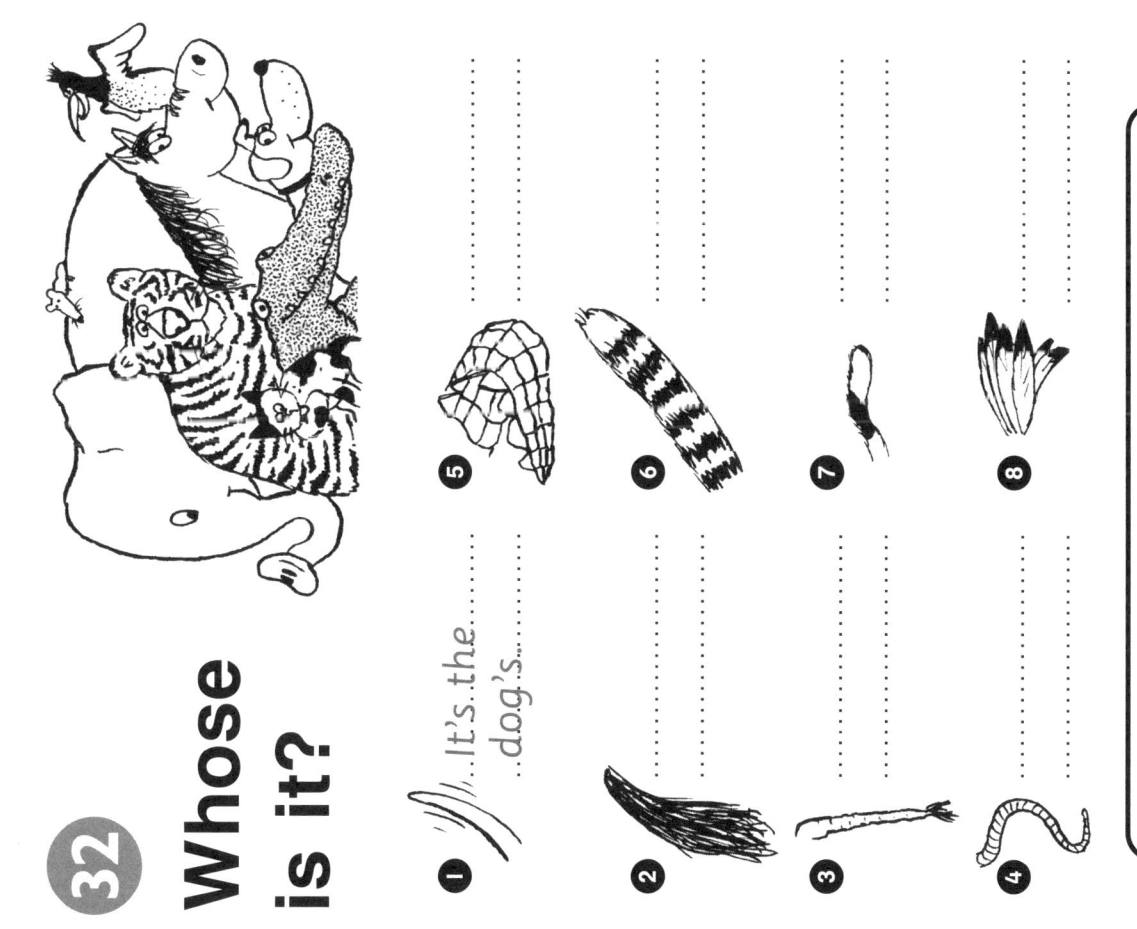

1. It's the dog's.
2. ....
3. ....
4. ....
5. ....
6. ....
7. ....
8. ....

mouse tiger elephant dog
cat bird horse crocodile

33 this, that, these, those

1. ....'s my school.
2. .... are my friends.
3. .... is my dog.
4. .... are my brothers.
5. ....'s good.
6. .... are good.

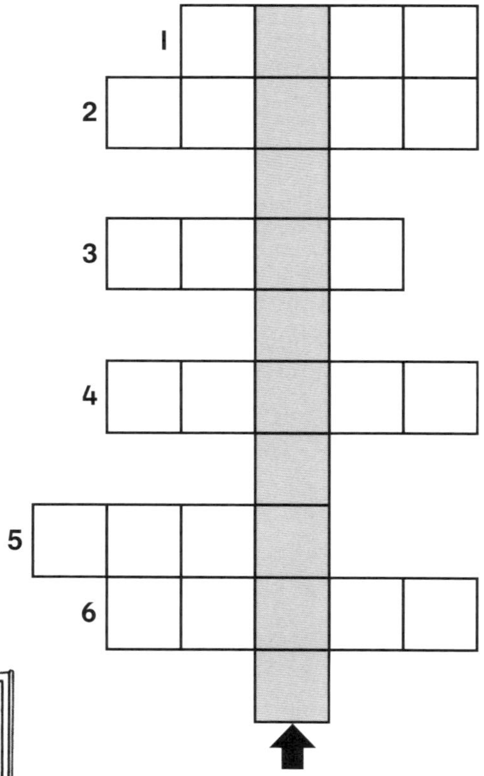

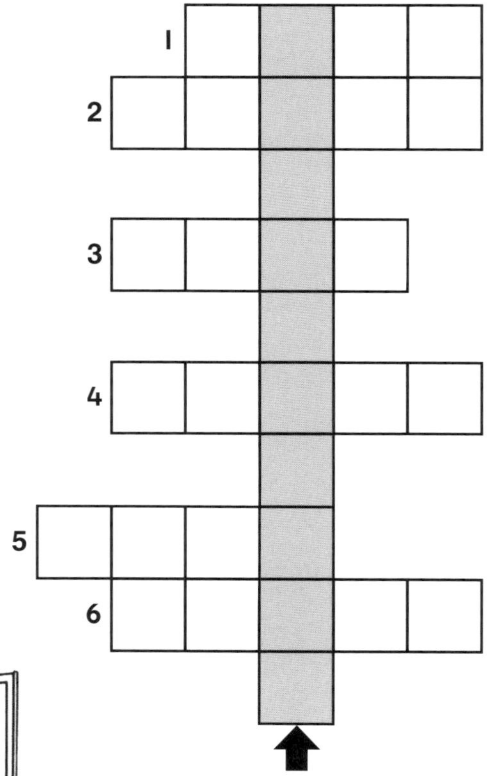

What's the word?

34 Zig which, what, who, whose, where

1. ...... are you? — I'm Zig.
2. ...... do you live?
3. ...... is yours? — That one.
3. ...... is that? — It's mine.
4. ...... 's your name? — I'm Tom.
5. ...... do you want?
6. ...... 's that? — It's a dog.

Thanks, Mother!

35

mouth	thanks	this	clothes
the	there	bath	with	they
birthday	mother	throw	three

36 Where's the bird?

```
i n c s y t x i h
u b e t w e e n p
b v r c d w z f a
n e p f m u m r l
e q h d g r e o n
x n h i v d s n k
t w j x n u t t y
t q k u j d v o e
o a f g l h z f j
```

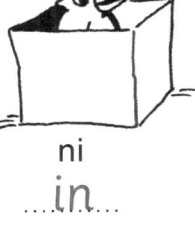

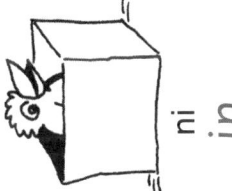

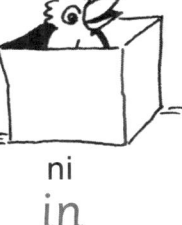

ni
in

ni tofrn fo

ebihdn

no

enebtwe

xnet ot

enudr

37 The word is ...

again very not there
today here now

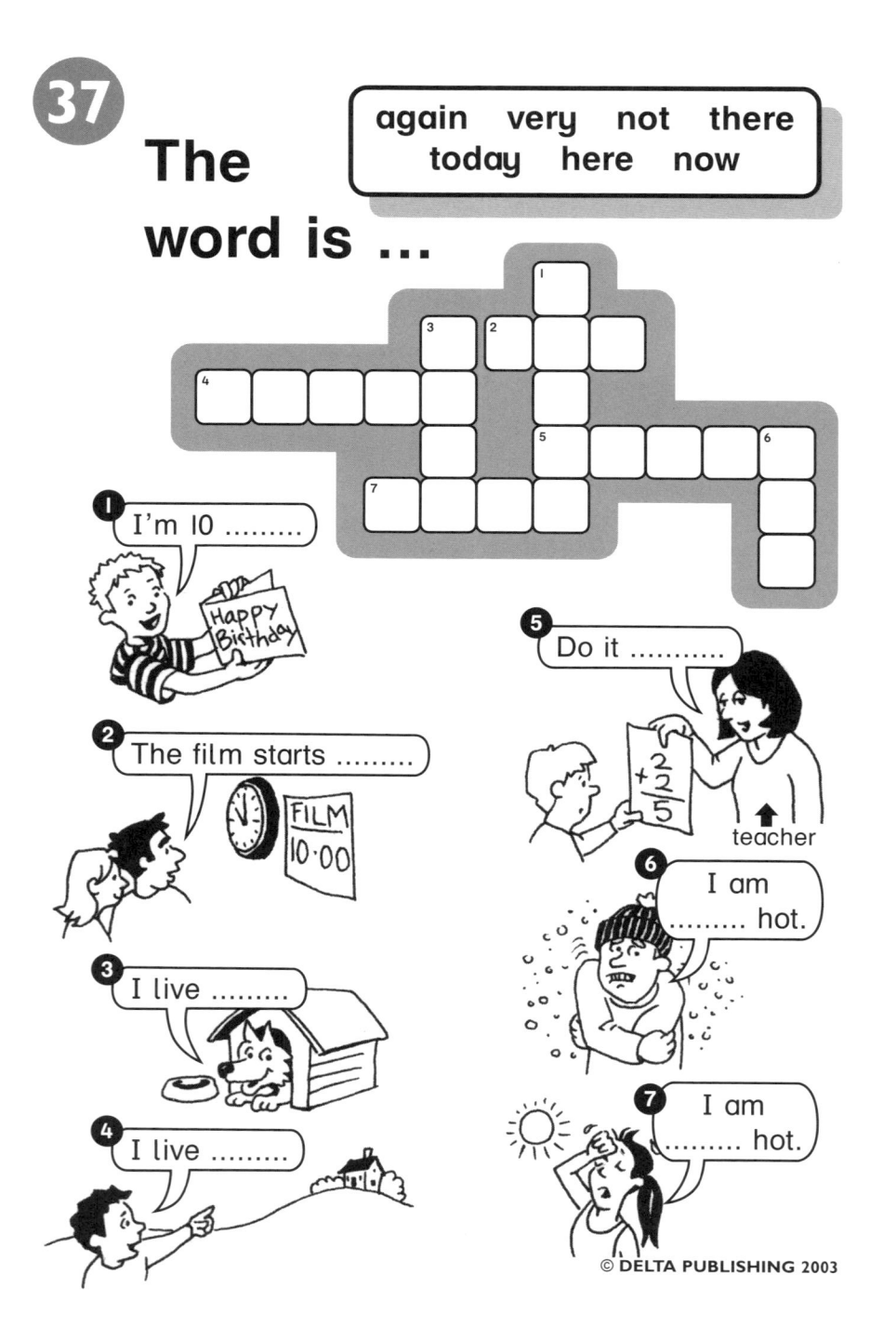

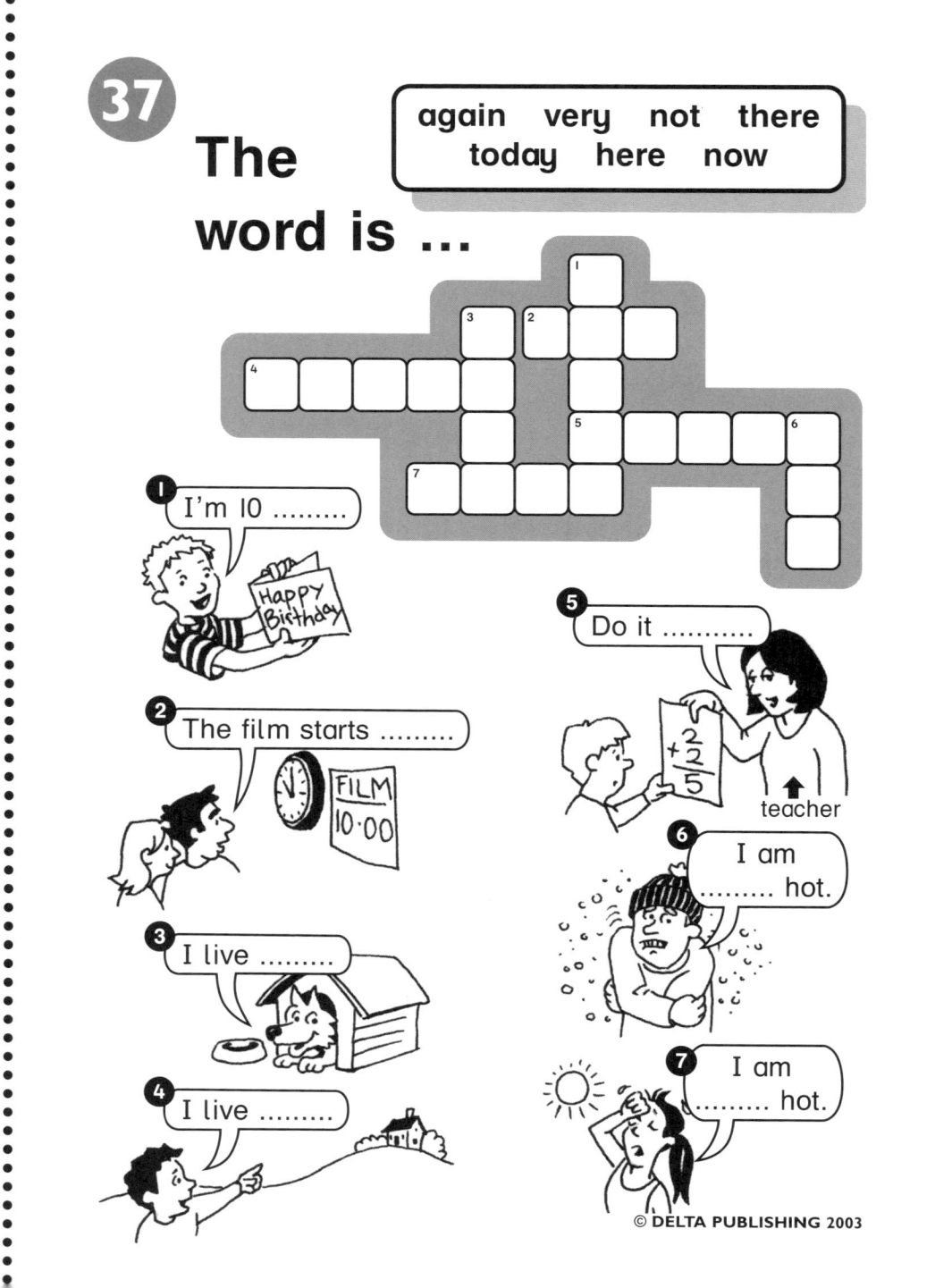

1. I'm 10 ....
2. The film starts ....
3. I live ....
4. I live ....
5. Do it ....
6. I am .... hot.
7. I am .... hot.

Grammar index

(**Numbers refer to the puzzle, not the page**)

adjectives **5, 7**

adverbs **37**

articles (*a/an/the*) **18, 31**

be **3**

can/can't **9, 10, 27, 28**

do/does **10, 18**

have got **7, 10, 18, 23, 27**

imperatives **14**

or **18**

plural *s* **6**

possessive *s* **8, 32**

prepositions of place **29, 36**

present continuous **13, 15, 20, 23, 27**

question forms **10, 18, 23, 27, 34**

simple present **3, 5, 10, 18**

some **18**

there is/there are **6, 15, 18**

these **23, 33**

this **16, 23, 33**

whose **23**

Topic index

alphabet **1**

adjectives **5, 7, 10, 25**

adverbs **37**

animals **6, 7, 10, 16, 29, 32**

body parts **11, 31**

classroom vocabulary **14, 15**

clothes **13, 15**

colours **4, 7, 15, 29**

family members **8**

food and drink **9, 22**

furniture **19, 21**

general vocabulary **2, 12, 16, 19, 24, 25, 26, 27**

household objects **21**

names **3, 5, 8, 9**

numbers **6**

prepositions **19, 29, 36**

questions and expressions **17, 27**

transport **19**

verbs **10, 15, 20, 25**

Also available:

puzzle time for movers

Photocopiable language activities for young learners who have completed around 100 hours learning. Includes puzzles on:

- comparatives
- superlatives
- the simple past
- the present continuous
- ordinal numbers (first, second, third, etc)
- prepositions of place
- must/mustn't

Follows the syllabus of Movers - level 2 of the Cambridge Young Learners English Tests.

puzzle time for flyers

Photocopiable language activities for young learners who have completed around 175 hours learning. Includes puzzles on:

- *going to*
- the present perfect
- the past continuous
- months of the year
- numbers up to 1,000
- *looks like, sounds like*, etc.
- *made of*

Follows the syllabus of Flyers - level 3 of the Cambridge Young Learners English Tests.

puzzle time for starters

Photocopiable language activities for young learners

Published by DELTA Publishing
Written by Jon Marks
Edited by Karen Gray
Designed by Peter Bushell
Cover artwork by Claire Mumford
Other artwork by Jon Marks and Claire Mumford

ADDRESS FOR CORRESPONDENCE:
Puzzle Time
DELTA Publishing
Quince Cottage
Hoe Lane
Peaslake
Surrey GU5 9SW
England

email: info@deltapublishing.co.uk
www.deltapublishing.co.uk

DELTA PUBLISHING

© DELTA PUBLISHING 2003. All rights reserved.

The photocopiable pages provided can be photocopied freely for use in the classroom and do not need to be declared.

Printed in the UK

ISBN 978-1-900783-71-2